PATIO AND WINDOWBOX GARDENING

TOM WELLSTED

NEW YORK

Editors: Susanne Mitchell
   & Pat Sinclair
Designer: John Fitzmaurice
Picture research:
   Moira McIlroy

Copyright © 1986 by
Marshall Cavendish Limited

First published in USA 1987
by Exeter Books
Distributed by Bookthrift
Exeter is a trademark of
Bookthrift Marketing Inc.
Bookthrift is a registered
trademark of Bookthrift
Marketing
New York, New York

ISBN 0-671-08441-0

Printed in Italy

CONTENTS

INTRODUCTION

PATIOS, OR YARDS, and window-boxes provide town gardeners, who may not possess a garden, with splendid opportunities for growing plants in easily maintained areas. However, those who do have a garden will also find that a patio, or terrace, makes an excellent additional feature, which is full of interest and color if well planted. It will be particularly useful for providing a solid base for decorative containers, barbecues, and garden furniture — and is very handy when the remainder of the garden is wet after a summer downpour.

A patio on good foundations, such as one on a hardcore bed, may be regarded as something of a flat rock garden, where many plants which require sharp drainage, alpines and figs for example, may grow and flourish. Most hardy decora-tive plants, the more tender annuals, even fruit and vegetables, will thrive if planted in suitable containers or in windowboxes. The restrictions of this type of gardening are provided by the plants themselves — their size, height and spread, or the numbers needed to make a good display or produce a reasonable crop — and the size of your containers. Large trees and massive, dense bushes are not going to be an asset to any patio, let alone a windowbox. Fortunately there are many, lovely, low, or slow-growing trees and shrubs which make ideal patio plants, and some are also good for windowboxes; as well as these there are hundreds of perennials, bulbs, annuals and delightful rock plants. Most patios have one side adjoining the house wall and this may be used for growing

climbing plants and wall shrubs, which will make a decorative backing to set off the patio. On large patios, other structures, such as arbors, pergolas and trellis arches, may be turned into a riot of color with suitable climbers. Frames for climbers, made from canes or trellis work, may be used in windowboxes, or other large windowsill based containers, but beware of making them too top heavy in windy weather when the frames are covered with leaves.

Apart from the fig already mentioned, there are other fruits and many vegetables which will grow surprisingly well when confined in troughs, tubs, pots and windowboxes. As with ornamental plants, large trees and shrubs should be avoided. There are many smaller growing fruiting plants, often of superior quality, which may be tried, including fine gooseberries, strawberries and the sweet cherry 'Stella' on a dwarfing rootstock. Herbs are splendid in containers and very easy to grow too. There is also a large range of suitable vegetables, particularly salad plants, which

may be raised in windowboxes and other containers, where the individual soil requirements are easily satisfied.

As well as the decorative value of the plants, patios may be made attractive features on their own. Windowbox decoration is somewhat limited but for patios there are many forms, colors and patterns of paving, the possible construction of low walled beds or low surrounding walls, as well as the almost limitless ranges of decorated containers and statuary. Even the usually brightly colored growing bags may be used and subdued by enclosing in a low wall of brick or wood. Growing bags may, in fact, be a very useful addition as, in conjunction with the growing bag plastic covers now available, they may be used as mini-greenhouses for the raising or growing on of some tender plants. Dramatic lighting, especially when reflected off a pool at night, adds yet another dimension. These are just a few of the many ideas which could make your patio an all year round delight. Borrow and adapt the best to suit your needs.

Above A bolder design where the diverse shapes of the plants' foliage break the starkness of the high, plain walls. The overhead trellis could support honeysuckle which would allow light to filter through to the seating area

CHAPTER ONE

PATIO DESIGN

Below and *opposite* By emphasizing different levels — with raised beds and with climbing plants and trees which cover the walls, you can make even the smallest corner into an intriguing, well stocked patio

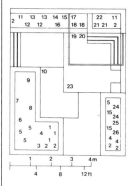

1 *Bergenia cordifolia*
2 *Berberis thunbergii*
3 *Epimedium x rubrum*
4 *Astilbe simplicifolia*
5 *Hosta fortunei*
6 *Iris sibirica*
7 *Hedera helix* 'Glacier'
8 *Rhus typhina*
9 *Rheum palmatum*
10 *Typha latifolia*
11 *Wistaria sinensis*
12 *Helianthemum*
13 *Acanthus mollis*
14 *Hedera helix*
15 *Potentilla fruticosa*
16 *Elaeagnus pungens*
17 *Lonicera japonica*
18 *Macleaya cordata*
19 *Hypericum patulum*
20 *Verbascum bombyciferum*
21 *Senecio laxifolius*
22 *Helichrysum splendidum*
23 *Hosta* 'Thomas Hogg'
24 *Cordyline australis*
25 *Hosta sieboldiana*
26 *Kniphofia uvaria*

PATIOS, IN THE modern sense of the word, are flat areas, usually paved, where it is possible to enjoy the outdoors in home surroundings and without getting muddy and soiled in wet weather. The firm base makes an ideal surface for garden furniture, for growing certain plants, for barbecue parties or just dining out or relaxing.

If you have not inherited a patio with your home, there are a number of considerations to be taken into account when planning the layout. First, you must decide on the type of paving. Then, do you want lighting, and if so what sort? Have you room for a pool and a fountain? Is your patio large enough to put up pergolas, or other structures, for climbing plants? These and other possibilities have to be thought out at the beginning; alterations made later can be costly. All this may also be applicable to an inherited patio, but at least in this case you can grow your plants in containers or

raised beds built on the existing surface. When planning a new patio, unpaved areas may be left as beds for plants.

Think of the patio as an extension of the home and plan its features in the same way as you would for the rooms in the home. It will quickly become apparent what you may or may not include in the area. Take note of the direction of the sun and if the patio is shaded in any way, such as by trees or other buildings. When working out how large an area you need, it will almost certainly be worth extending your original idea for too small an area may lead to much frustration later. Before you start work, draw a rough plan not only of the patio but also of its surrounds — home, garden, walls and trees, which may be in the vicinity. They will all affect your layout. Try sitting and standing on the site too, so that you judge properly how high to build a screening wall, or which plants will look well against this backdrop.

Above This city patio with its beautiful old stone and fig tree surrounded by pebbles, looks distinctive seen from either end of the garden

1 *Artemisia absinthium*
2 *Magnolia grandiflora*
3 *Lonicera x tellmanniana*
4 *Berberis thunbergii*
5 *Clematis montana*
6 *Sedum maximum*
7 *Rosa* 'Iceberg'
8 *Ajuga reptans*
9 *Garrya elliptica*
10 *Macleaya cordata*
11 *Helianthemum*
12 *Acanthus mollis*
13 *Cytisus scoparius*
14 *Rosa* 'Z. Drouhin'
15 *Vitis coignetiae*
16 *Fuchsia magellanica*

17 *Robinia pseudoacacia*
18 *Lamium galeobdolon*
19 *Pyracantha angustifolia*
20 *Hosta sieboldiana*
21 *Galtonia candicans*
22 *Euphorbia robbiae*
23 *Helleborus argutifolius*
24 *Choisya ternata*
25 *Alchemilla mollis*
26 *Clematis armandii*
27 *Fatsia japonica*
28 *Ficus carica*
29 *Euphorbia wulfenii*
30 *Jasminum nudiflorum*
31 *Rosa* 'New dawn'
32 *Cordyline australis*

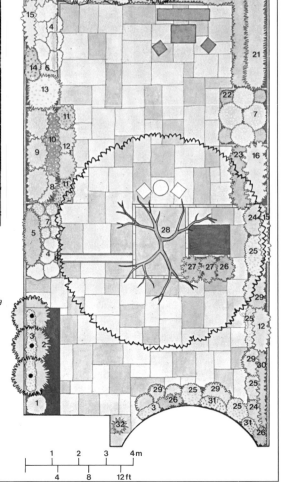

The Patio Surface

The surface of your patio is important since you will probably have to live with it for a long time. The foundation is even more important. Whatever you place on top may become uneven and sink or rise in places, making the patio a dangerous area to walk on. The base may simply be very well compacted ground covered with a layer of sand. The sand should not be less than 2in deep, and, if the ground does not slope by about 2in in every 30ft away from your house, make sure that the sand does to allow for drainage. Better than sand on hard ground is a hardcore based patio. Bear in mind that building regulations probably require that the patio surface should be at least 6in below the house dampcourse, so dig out the required area to a depth that allows for 3in of hardcore, which should then be rammed down or rolled hard, and 1in or so of sand and also whatever thickness of paving you have chosen. If an exceptionally strong base is required, to carry heavy loads such as a car, place the paving on a bed of mortar using 6 parts sand to 1 part cement; for ordinary paving use a mix of 9 to 1 putting a dab at each corner and one at the center of each slab. Or ask your building dealer for advice.

Paving

Paving stones are now available in a range of artificial materials, usually concrete based, and in a wide range of colors, textures and shapes. It is usually best not to mix too many different types in one patio, two, in fact, generally being sufficient. The artificial paving is generally more durable than many of the natural stone slabs.

Stones can be attractive if they are laid down in areas between paving slabs or round the base of a small dramatic tree. Wood is also attractive but may be attacked by pests and diseases, which generally leads to the wood rotting away unless controlled by chemicals.

Whatever paving you choose, make sure that major features are either in place before you lay the paving or allow space for them. Any electric cables or water pipes should be laid first.

Once laid, the paving should need little attention apart from the occasional hose down and brush off. If slime and algae

are a problem there are now some good cleaning products available.

Bricks

If the idea of artificial paving made to simulate a brick surface does not appeal to you then, of course, there is no reason why the genuine material should not be used. Bricks come in a variety of colors and sizes but generally speaking they are best laid unmixed, in one type only. However, attractive features may be made with panels of a different colored brick or brick size; the last will require some

Above Patterned ceramic tiles are used widely in the countries bordering the Mediterranean. A simple black and white pattern avoids too cluttered an appearance

Right Paving options: A mix of concrete slabs, brick and stones (top), and stone slabs and bricks weathered to a uniform tone (below). *Far right* Loose gravel and stepping stones (top) and a radiating pattern made with bricks and stones (below)

Below Stones eliminate weeding work and add variety to a paved area which might otherwise be monotonous

planning to make sure that the different sizes will fit together. Whatever you choose, lay the bricks on edge for the longest life. There is no need to set them in a plain end to end ribbon either; set at an angle of 45 degrees, very attractive herringbone patterns may be made, either over the whole patio or as a central or edging strip.

Gravel

Gravel makes an inexpensive patio covering. It is, however, rather mobile if heavy use is made of the patio and the least supportive of surfaces when furniture is placed upon it. There are many plants which will greatly appreciate the rapid drainage that it gives, in particular the rock garden types such as aethionemas, anacyclus, erinus, portulaca, sedums and sempervivums, to name a few of those recommended in the chapter on ornamental plants. Pea gravel is probably the most satisfactory for size and color and its round profile will not damage furniture or feet so much as the sharp, granitic grits. The latter are available in natural grays and white as well as artificially colored forms. The colored forms are not to be recommended as they will often clash with the flowers or foliage. If you wish for a more solid support than that provided by an all

over gravel patio, then insets made by leaving out a paving stone and filling the area with gravel will give an alternative texture to the patio, whether the gravel panel is planted up or not.

Patio Beds

In addition to gravel panels set into paved patios, other permanent beds should be considered. These provide growing spaces, which although permanent do not require the regular renewal of soil or synthetic mixes as movable containers do and, by being incorporated into the patio design, should not clutter up the patio surface. According to size, anything that can be grown in a container can be planted in patio beds from the larger shrubs, such as abutilons, to the small summer display plants, such as salvia and tagetes.

Unless you have a very large patio, it is best to keep such beds to the surrounds and they are particularly effective when used against, or built into, a surrounding wall; or, again where large patios are concerned, they may be incorporated into a dividing wall. The height of this may be from just above ground level — the patio floor in this case — up to 3 ft or so, but take care because too tall a walled bed will dominate the patio.

Left Granite setts and concrete slabs (top) and in similar design, imitation stone — concrete slabs with rows of bricks (below). *Far left* Plants growing through gravel soften its appearance (top), and bricks interrupted with lines of wood and slate add to the texture of the paving (below)

Below A low, solid wall does double duty as seating and as raised area for sun-seeking plants such as these potted tomatoes. The weathered brick, used also for paving, gives continuity to the design, and, invaded by the grass, integrates well with the rest of the garden

Pools

Pools are, all too often, placed in the middle of a patio, and again this is fine if you have either a little used or very large patio. But generally such a position is a disaster because the pool is a fixture and will get in the way of all the other patio

Right A tiny pool can be an effective focal point if treated boldly like this one with its striking fountain

Below Precision-laid brickwork and concrete slabs create a pool of rectangular dimensions in harmony with the clean lines of this patio

pleasures — sitting, eating, sunbathing, growing plants, having barbecues and so on. Set to one side, however, the pool becomes a valuable feature and this is even more true if you are able to position it partly in sun and partly in shade. Most fish and aquatic plants will appreciate this, so build a low wall to one side if necessary. Alternatively, consider building a permanent wall seat if the shading wall is not part of a patio surrounding wall.

There are various moulded pools on the market, often in bright blue or light gray and these colors will always give an unnatural effect. Pool liners of butyl, and the butyl substitute plastics with a black finish, will give not only a more natural appearance but will also last longer. They are, however, a bit more expensive and you will have to dig out the pool shape. But this means you can decide upon the shape and number of ledges or shelves yourself. Whichever pool system you choose, make sure that the rim is below the patio surface so that the pool's surrounding stones or paving are level with the patio. This will also prevent the pool from flooding the patio unless there is an exceptionally heavy overflow due to some mishap.

Walls and Hedges

A surrounding wall around the patio may provide some shade for your pool. It also sets the patio off and gives it an air of distinction as well as providing protection from wind for human and plant inhabitants. For this purpose a solid wall should not be too high or you may get a down-draught in windy conditions. If you do wish for a high surround then, as with a garden, a hedge which will filter the wind will be much better. Solid surrounds include brick walls, lapped wooden fencing, especially strengthened glass or rigid plastic. Wooden fencing, if woven, will allow some wind to filter through but, as with lapped wooden fencing, it requires regular maintenance and painting with a wood preservative, and a check should be kept on its stability. Hedging plants may need regular clipping unless they are dwarf species but by using a plant such as the 'Skyrocket' juniper, clipping is kept to the minimum for years, and indeed may not be necessary at all. Other fine hedging plants are found in some berberis, escallonias and rugosa roses.

Above left Lush vegetation softens the edges of this dark, teardrop pool, while *below* the plants in this clear-cut pool emphasize the restrained style of the patio. *Above* The timber is heavy duty but complements the pool by following its outline

Right It is worth considering lighting a patio with individual lamps attaching them to walls or placing them in plant beds

Below Two contrasting scenes: a small patio lit discreetly with hidden lamps, and strong, colored illumination flooding an airy, open patio

Lighting

Lighting will increase the use of the patio, extending its useful hours on warm but dark evenings. Good lighting will also make the patio a feature to look out onto from the house. As most patios have at least one wall adjoining the house, the simplest form of lighting is supplied by a wall light, but this will not necessarily be the most attractive. All sorts of standard lamps are now available, in various plastics, plastic-coated metal, metal and concrete. Strings of lamps and parasol lights, twin or single, may also be used. Colored lights may be effective for a while but may also put a strain on the eyes if you are sitting under them for long periods. They are certainly effective as a feature, such as lighting a pool, if used in conjunction with other plain lights for the main patio illumination.

Do remember that electricity is dangerous and installations should be professionally fitted, especially if running off full mains power. Many pool lighting sets run from transformers, which are much safer, delivering the power at a lower voltage.

In addition to electric light, various gas lights are obtainable as well as flares. These may give rather an old world atmosphere with their more flickering

light but the latter can be dangerous if in the way of playing children or placed too near inflammable plastics.

Furniture

Almost any furniture suitable for gardens will look well on a patio, the hard surface providing a firm base for thinner legged furniture which might otherwise sink into a lawn. Furniture made from wood, plastic, resin, aluminum and iron, canvas covered or not, according to taste, will go well. Generally speaking, however, the plainer the lines with the least mix of colors is best. Multicolored canvas and bright painted furniture are fine on holiday but may become very wearisome when seen day in and day out. This is particularly true if the main color on your patio is provided by plants. With colorful plants around it is generally best to stick to one color for the furniture, preferably light or white, natural woods or plain tones.

It is possible to pay a great deal of money for a garden seat but fortunately there are very many excellent, and cheaper, seats, chairs, benches and tables. Durability is found in good wood, such as oak. It is heavy and may be plain or painted — painted oak, however, almost always peels after a while. Softer woods require constant attention if they are to last, and should be painted or treated with preservative annually. Plastic coated iron or steel furniture is heavy and unlike the light plastic coated aluminum, unlikely to get blown about in the wind. It is more costly than plastic but many plastic items deteriorate rather quickly and so need replacing more frequently. Resin furniture is also more expensive than plastic but longer lasting and generally of a better standard of design and in pleasant colors, and though comparable to light wood in weight, longer lasting than that too. Unlike the painted metals, the color is fast and resin furniture should be virtually maintenance free. Woven chairs of rattan cane are surprisingly long lasting and are light and attractive but will have to be kept under cover in poor weather. The modern alternative of woven nylon is also light and less susceptible to poor weather. Rattan may be painted to suit

Above Unpainted wooden furniture, like this unusual sofa sitting permanently on a rooftop patio, will benefit from a seasonal application of linseed oil. An annual coating of preservative will protect furniture from the weather

Right A canvas and wood 'director's chair' which tilts back makes comfortable as well as practical seating outdoors. As a folding chair it saves space as does the slatted table which is semi-circular

the owner's wishes. Some furniture elegantly combines rattan, for the frame, and woven nylon, for the back and seat.

Sunbeds and loungers made of plastic, resin or metal and synthetic cloths have largely replaced the canvas-covered, wooden deck chair. The loungers may come in sets with matching upholstery or are available as single items. Easily portable, very light loungers and sunbeds are made with tubular metal frames from which the bed sheet is suspended by springs.

There are a number of ranges of co-ordinated furniture offered and some saving may be possible by buying such sets. Typically these ranges comprise four chairs, a table and a parasol, the loungers, if available in the range, being additional items. Some ranges have chairs and seats with two rear wheels for ease of movement. Many are supplied with a choice of coordinated cushion, parasol and tablecloth fabrics, of cotton, dralon or synthetic weatherproof material. The cheaper plastic coverings are liable to split after a time and are rarely worthwhile buying in preference to the slightly more expensive fabrics. Fortunately these fabrics are now available in discrete and attractive designs which should harmonise well with most settings.

Tables are available with solid tops of marble, iron, aluminium or wood, as well as plastic and resin, and with slatted tops of wood or resin. Shapes and designs vary from round to oval and square to rectangular, some with drop leaves and others with centre extensions for large parties. Parasols may be incorporated into the table design, either with a central hole being left for the parasol stick with the stick fitted into an integral base. A popular design is a combined unit of table and two benches made of light or heavy wood.

As well as the vast range of tables and seats, other accessory furniture includes trolleys, side tables, swinging hammocks and stools. Trolleys are very useful for conveying meals, drinks, books and papers, and other leisure items from the house to the sitting area. Folding stools, too, are useful extras, taking up little space when stored but providing that extra seat for the unexpected visitor.

Furnishing Accessories

Flower pot stands, awnings, trellises, arbors and archways as well as a variety of decorative statuary, will all help to give your patio a 'lived-in' appearance. But do keep everything practical.

Awnings will provide a welcome sun shade over the door or French window leading onto a terrace or patio yard. If you already have a coordinated set of furniture it is worth seeing if, as is sometimes the case, awning coverings to match are also available. If not, as near as possible a match is better than some violent contrast. It can be quite jarring to see some obviously otherwise well thought out patio and furnishing plan upset by one prominent feature being out of style. A plain color, preferably matching one of those in the rest of the furniture, will often be the best choice.

Flower pot stands range from simple urns to figures or elaborate, multi-armed structures looking rather like giant candelabras. The latter need careful siting and are definitely not to all tastes as they have a strong Victorian look about them. Statues and animal figures abound. Some are so designed to hold a pot, usually at arm's length, but others are decorative in their own right. What suits your patio will need careful consideration. Stone or synthetic stone and lead are the traditional materials. To these are now added glass fiber, moulded plastic and resin, which are usually finished to resemble stone or lead but are lighter in weight and a great deal less expensive.

House walls may be covered with trellis for climbing plants. If so, it is best to have a solid framed structure, hinged at the base, so that it may easily be pulled outwards to allow for painting or re-

pointing. Wire trellis is also used for arches and arbors. These are attractive additions if you have space, excellent for climbing plants, whether lovely roses or luscious grapes. Large patios may be partially surrounded by a series of such arches or a solid posted pergola may be preferred. Whatever structure is put up, do make sure that it is firmly anchored. The modern arbors and arches are usually made of steel rods and wire mesh coated with plastic. They should last a long time.

A sundial or a pedestalled bird bath can make an interesting focal point on a patio with little else in it, relieving the plainness and providing a trouble-free ornament. Sundials may even be used to give a rough idea of the time, while a regularly filled bird bath should be a source of pleasure all year round.

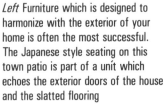

Left Furniture which is designed to harmonize with the exterior of your home is often the most successful. The Japanese style seating on this town patio is part of a unit which echoes the exterior doors of the house and the slatted flooring

Left Plastic coated metal furniture is lightweight and virtually weatherproof. The hinged seats and fold away table under this shelter are designed to save space, but, remaining in their position, make an attractive feature on the patio

Right A bench built with materials used elsewhere on the patio integrates well into the overall design. Stone or brick seating covered with naturally finished wood blends in with most settings

Cold frames

The flat surface of a patio provides an ideal base for a cold frame. This offers a convenient facility for raising and acclimating many plants. It may also be used to cover more tender plants in adverse weather or used during the warmer months for growing salad crops. Cold frames are available in a variety of materials. Most modern ones are made of a light framework of sectional strip metal. Glazing may be of glass but more usually of clear plastic or other transparent or translucent material, which may be rigid or stretched film. Glass is probably still the best material from the plants' point of view, but has the disadvantages of easy breakage and weight. The low breaking point is, of course, of importance where there are children, but it does not break down in strong sun.

Glass used to be the traditional material too and some remarkably cumbersome and dangerous contraptions were made using it. Most modern cloches — mini-greenhouses — are light and easy to use, being made of lightweight plastics. There are cloches made of stout wire frames covered with heavy gauge plastic bags. These make good covers for large pots or urns, or several may be used close together in a half tub, for example. The bags will last several years and are easily replaced. One new cloche is specially designed to cover growing bags, is a cross between a typical cloche and a small cold frame. It is made of twin-skin plastic sheet with high light admission.

Barbecues

Despite the general variability of our climate, barbecues are increasingly popular. If you are starting from scratch, it is worth considering building a permanent brick barbecue into the patio structure. Custom-made barbecues make attractive additions to a patio and may be large, small or double units according to the likely needs. They may be built round, square, rectangular or indeed to any design you like, and placed so as to fit in with the overall patio design.

Portable barbecues are, however, by far the most popular, and there are plenty of designs and price ranges to choose from. Which to choose is obviously a matter of personal choice but one point to remember is that many people choose one too small for their needs. If there are several people to feed it is worth getting a barbecue slightly larger than you think you need.

Though not absolutely necessary, many people prefer barbecues with windshields. These are certainly good in fairly calm conditions but a good wind will get round them too. Spits are another possibility. They may be hand turned but are a real advantage when motorized,

either with a mechanical unit or electric motor. One option that should be looked for is a system which allows the grill to be raised or lowered above the charcoal so that the heat may be varied once the charcoal is ready. In the case of barbecues running off gas cylinders this is not necessary as the strength of flame may be varied.

Above Circular in shape and made of concrete, like the raised pool, this barbecue is a built-in feature compatible with a modern, streamlined garden

Left Barbecues made of bricks with a metal plate and wire grill are easy to construct. Additional storage space for wood, charcoal and cooking utensils is worth considering

CHAPTER TWO

CONTAINERS AND WINDOWBOXES

Opposite A delightful display of fuchsias and lobelias spilling over a floor mounted windowbox which is surrounded by the drooping stems of passion flower

Below Concrete containers, once weathered and sensitively planted up, can often resemble stone, and will look good against natural materials used on the patio

ONCE, APART FROM gardens themselves, clay pots, half tubs and urns, made of stone or metal, were all there was for growing plants in. Now, with the development of many different plastic and fiber materials, a huge range of different sized, shaped and textured containers is available. Most of these modern materials are much lighter and, when some of the larger containers have to be moved, this is a real advantage.

TYPES OF CONTAINER

Most common, and far from objectionable, are the modern plastic pots, troughs and planters. In the smaller sizes there is more or less no alternative to straightforward plant pots. Most follow the design of the conventional clay pot, though various other colors are available, particularly green, brown and black. Breaking away from the standard form is a new pot which is made of black plastic and bought in a flat pack. For use, the sides are bent up and clip into each other to make a pot with a narrower top than base. The design is good for stability and excellent for plant removal. Its greatest advantage, however, is probably in ease of storage — of some importance to town gardeners with perhaps only a small patio or windowbox and no garden shed.

Larger sizes of pot or planter are usually made in subdued colored plastic which shows the plants off to advantage. The plastic may be plain and shiny, with a matt texture or textured to simulate stone, or finished to resemble old lead containers. Wood grain is another attractive finish. There are also plastic containers with a self-watering system incorporated into the design.

Glass fiber troughs, pots and planters are very light and usually moulded to resemble stone or metal. Moulded cellulose fiber, which is bonded with resins and resembles peat-made pots, is another light alternative. Unlike the plastics and glass fiber, it absorbs moisture and has been assessed as much more difficult to overwater. These patio planters have a much shorter life too, about two years, a fact which at least ensures that a perennial plant grown in one should get a reasonably frequent change of soil. Unfortunately they give little protection against frost.

Genuine stone and lead containers are extremely expensive, heavy and awkward items. Hardly less expensive

Above The lax appearance of *Begonia* 'Midas' perfectly complements the elegance of this free-standing container

Below A colorful riot of blooms supported by cement containers, a terracotta tub and hanging wire baskets

and almost as heavy are some of the concrete or stone composition reproductions. They come in a wide range of sizes and heights.

Terracotta has the warmest color of all the unpainted, non-plastic containers. The clay is moulded into a number of sizes and designs, from large urns to small troughs, and in a variety of saucer shapes. The saucers have a space age look about them, particularly the larger sizes of 3ft or so diameter, and are usually plain. Troughs and urns may have antique-style scrolls, faces or leaf and grape bunch mouldings on one or more sides. The material is fairly light when dry but becomes quite heavy when damp, and slightly darker in color. Terracotta containers blend in well with all surroundings and the earthy color sets off plants to advantage and is probably the best choice for darker leaved plants, and blue flowers. Protect these containers from hard frosts.

Container size

What size container to use will depend on what is planted in it. To use pot sizes as an example, most alpines, many annual plants and young perennial plants and shrubs are bought in small pots of 3–5in diameter, and up to about 8in for camellias and rhododendrons. Inevitably, at the time of purchase these will already be too small for the plants growing in them. Transfer bedding plants to a pot about 2in larger, or if putting several plants into a container, allow a similar increase in growing space.

For permanent plantings more individual requirements have to be considered. For instance, camellias may be transferred to their final pot size of 10in, fuchsias to 8in, and left to grow on for a year or two. A larger size of pot will always be better than a smaller as it will afford greater protection for the roots in winter and in summer will not dry out so quickly. The sheer weight of the greater volume of moist soil is also an advantage in keeping the plant firmly on the ground in windy spells. Clump-forming perennials, whether ornamental or culinary, should also be planted in much larger containers than you might think necessary, to allow for their spread, or you will continually be having to pot them on.

Dwarf, slow-growing conifers, which are not clump forming, may be content for several years in a 6–7in pot, or several of them in a larger container. On the other hand, wide-spreading conifers, such as the creeping juniper, are best planted into a bed as they become very difficult to pot on and water when their container is completely obscured.

Pot covers

Plain pots may always be disguised in pot covers made of plastic, china or, more expensively, in reproductions of Victorian cast iron work. The modern versions fortunately have a corrosion resistant coating. Other pot covers are made of wood or wickerwork. Such plant covers are very useful for temporary schemes or for potted plants which are brought indoors for the winter. Pot covers allow flexibility, enabling plants to be interchanged without potting.

As an alternative to using such containers you can always make your own. A container made of bricks may be varied

in design, according to your needs. Unless it is very large, particularly in height, no mortar will be needed, in fact permanently built raised beds may be too inflexible for the patio area. Attractive schemes may be laid out with several beds adjoining, especially if these have different wall heights.

Arranging containers

Having made your selection of containers, using them to get the best effect is another matter. Random placement without a scheme in mind will inevitably result in an untidy appearance, and, as the plants grow, the containers will probably need a good deal of moving round to avoid obscuring other plants or features.

For similar reasons, putting a row of planted pots around the whole patio is going to look odd unless the sizes of pot and potential sizes of the plants are carefully arranged to give a wave-like flow. It is usually more satisfactory to make a feature of a group of containers of different sizes, putting the lowest at the front, and to plant them up so that as the plants grow they do not obscure one another. In fact, with well staggered pot sizes, the plants themselves may be of much the same size — the height differential coming from their containers. Try a group of five containers of three different heights, the largest to the rear of the main viewpoint, two slightly smaller ones to one side and two smaller still to the other. Or use plants of similar size set at different levels.

An arrangement like this will give a controlled yet casual look and makes a good corner site feature if planted up with the tallest plants at the back in the largest containers, then graduating through medium-sized ones to a few

trailers in the front. Too many containers in a group will give a rather heavy appearance. Smaller groups, even three pots of two sizes, repeated several times, will be of more interest.

Troughs

Troughs are good for corner work as well as for bordering a patio. As a corner ornamentation, a group of three troughs, suitably staggered, can look very attractive. Alternatively, try a square container in the corner flanked by two troughs. Most troughs may be used as window boxes too. Tubs, or rather half tubs, make excellent containers capable of holding many plants. Large containers do not have to contain large plants of course. Indeed large containers, such as sinks or half tubs, are the ideal place for an alpine plant collection. The sinks can be made to blend with more natural surroundings if dressed with a peat and cement mix which disguises the shiny white porcelain. Whatever you do with your sink, do remember to leave the plug hole open and put in a layer of drainage material to provide an outlet for surplus water. This is very important if you are using the sink for alpines that require rapid drainage such as dryas, lewisias and saxifrages, annuals such as portulaca and mesembryanthemum, or perhaps a collection of thymes. The drainage layer, which needs to be about 2in deep, may be of small stones or coarse grit.

Growing Bags

Growing bags are a convenient modern form of container mostly used for growing tomatoes and other vegetable crops. The mix is peat based and the plastic bag ensures minimum evaporation and prevents it drying out too rapidly. Because of this, growing bags are best used for plants with a heavy water demand such as tomatoes, sweet peppers and lettuces among the vegetables but are equally good for ornamental plants with similar needs, such as begonias, polyanthus and the trailing *Thunbergia fragrans* 'Angel Wings'.

The disadvantage is that the colors of the growing bag plastic may clash with the flowers, in which case the bags may be enclosed in another plain bag, or be partially disguised behind a low brick or stone wall.

Left Troughs are excellent for temporary displays of summer flowers, besides evergreen plants. If movable they offer great flexibility with planting schemes

Below Growbags solve the problem of raising plants in restricted space where, perhaps, no garden soil is available. They are acceptable for plants which need plenty of water

WINDOWBOXES

Windowboxes are containers which are specially made to fit on to window ledges but any other container which also fits on the ledge may be used for the same purpose. They are made of exactly the same materials as other containers: imitation stone, terracotta, metal, assorted plastics and wood. Wood will eventually rot though it may take a few years to do so. The rot usually begins at the base or at side fixings, unless the box is used for annual plantings only and cleaned out each year and treated with a modern wood preservative which does not harm plants. The other materials will generally last longer but some plastics discolor and become brittle. Unfortunately the acid in the atmosphere will gradually attack metal even if you take the trouble to line a metal windowbox. The combination of acid and weather will also gradually erode stone and terracotta but it takes longer than with the other materials.

Securing the box

Weight must also be considered. Even the lightest plastic windowbox when filled with moist soil and a few plants will be quite heavy. Weight is an advantage since it helps to hold the windowbox on the ledge, but make sure that your window ledge is sound and able to take it. Additional fixing is recommended, however, to prevent the box slipping off. This need not involve heavy structural work. One of the simplest ways is to take advantage of the need to provide a space between the bottom of the box and the ledge for drainage, by using two or three mild steel brackets, one arm of each screwed firmly to the ledge so that the other arm sticks up at the outer edge of the ledge in the front, with a similarly fixed bracket at each side. This will hold most boxes against accidental knocking off or slipping. The brackets may be painted to blend with the box and wall or ledge. More decorative are specially made metal surrounds, like miniature balcony rails, but more movement may be possible within their confines, and then some way of tethering the box or containers will be needed.

Brackets may also be used, where practicable, to fix windowboxes directly to the house wall, making sure that the wall fixing is absolutely sound and the screws will not be pulled out by forward movement of the box. Drill any holes in plastic and terracotta with great care so as not to damage and crack the material. As an extra precaution when bolting the arm of the bracket to the box, use a washer to prevent cracking as you tighten on each side — so that you get a sandwich of bracket, washer, box and washer held together by the bolt head and nut. Tap washers are quite suitable.

Before fixing your box and planting it up, make sure that there is a gap between the box bottom and the ledge of at least ½in to allow excess water to run off. Use replaceable wooden chocks or metal box sections of about ¾in wide by the width of the box, about one such support for every 12in of box length. Generally, the size of box is determined by the length of window ledge available but there is no reason why two or more boxes to each ledge are not used, provided that they are adequately fixed.

Using several boxes has the advantage that they can be planted up to give their best displays at different times, or a permanently planted box may be flanked by two annually planted boxes. The only disadvantage is that the smaller the container the more attention it will require with regard to watering and fertilizing.

The commercially produced window-

Below A — Metal shelf brackets bent upwards and attached to the wall will hold a windowbox in place
B — Wooden battens are attached to the bottom of the box to raise it above any standing water on the ledge
C — If your window ledge is not at a right angle to the wall, angled battens can be used to wedge the box in position

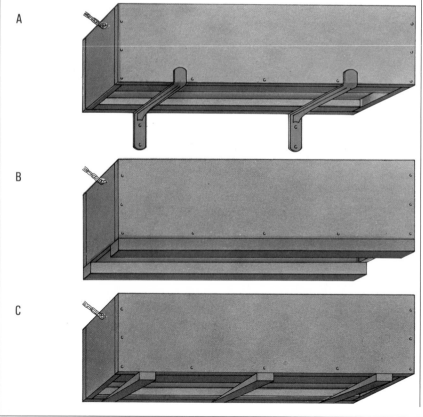

A

B

C

Left Lobelias, sweet alyssums, chrysanthemums, and geraniums will live happily in the same box, providing a colorful summer display

Below Slightly more subdued this red, white and blue theme uses geraniums, fuchsias, lobelias and variegated English ivies

Left Ideal for a winterbox is a mix of dwarf conifers, and English ivy. If pruned to prevent it smothering the other plants euonymous will add lighter colors to the planting scheme

boxes are available in sizes ranging from 5×6×19in to the much larger, depending on the box material, of about 8½ × 11½ × 59in); custom made boxes may be of any size to suit your window ledge and such boxes are usually made of wood.

Container soil

The soil used should be just the same as for any other container, moisture retentive but free draining. It has always been customary to add a layer of rubble, broken crocks or other free-draining material to the bottom before filling with the potting mix, but provided care is taken not to overwater, this is rarely necessary except in areas where the boxes may be exposed to high rainfall. And here a 1in covering of pea gravel will reduce compaction. Soil-based mixes are easier to manage, but are heavier than peat-based formulas.

Modern peat-based mixes should be sufficiently free draining on their own, but if there is any doubt about the drainage capability it is better to amend the soil by adding about 10 per cent by volume of coarse sand, rather than restrict the growing depth. It is always worth taking a lot of care with windowbox displays because they are often enjoyed by people who do not have gardens.

Below The large blooms of begonias with the smaller geraniums, and delicate flowers of sweet alyssums and lobelias make a strong summer display

Above A windowbox capturing the spirit of spring, including daffodils, crocus, scilla, wallflowers and forget-me-nots with trailing English ivy

Below After the warm seasons' show substitute dwarf conifers and ericas. Cotoneasters will add late color, with sedums and sempervivum forming mats

Above Another option for summer is a selection of plants such as marguerites, petunias, marigolds, and the ivy leaved geranium and ageratum

HANGING BASKETS

Hanging baskets, and half baskets for wall mounting, may be made in the traditional way by lining a wire basket with moss and filling it with potting mix. A much quicker and easier way is to use a moulded fiber liner, which is placed in the wire basket and filled with potting mix. Wire baskets, too, have been largely replaced by baskets of plastic mesh or plastic-coated wire, as well as moulded plastic bowls, and some of these incorporate drip trays as part of the design. Watch out for drips from windowsill containers; make sure the latter are firmly fixed.

Planting schemes

The planting up of hanging baskets and windowboxes follows the same principles. Generally taller growing plants should be central, or just to one side of center to give an asymmetrical design, with lower growing plants in diminishing size towards the edges or ends, and finishing up with trailing plants at the container's edge. A simple, permanent scheme might consist of a central miniature rose, such as 'Baby Faurax', which is surrounded by the dark-leaved *Ophiopogon* 'Nigrescens' and with a grayish leaved English ivy trailing from the edges, such as *Hedera* 'Glacier'.

In complete contrast, you might prefer a brilliant annual summer display scheme, with the centre taken by a fiery scarlet salvia, surrounded by an intense band of yellow and mahogany tagetes, the hot colors being emphasized by the cool blue of a trailing lobelia at the edges. Both these schemes have plant height gradation and plant form variation and use very different leaves or flowers. Such contrasts will improve the design of your planting scheme and make a far more interesting basket.

Above To plant up a hanging basket first line it with plastic, and puncture small drainage holes in the bottom. Fill with potting mix and make slits at intervals passing the root balls of the plants through from the outside of the basket into the soil

Left Mixed fuchsias in hanging baskets give spark to an otherwise unremarkable garden fence

27

CHAPTER THREE

PLANT CARE

Opposite Stunning blooms of pendulous and tuberous begonias frame a patio window, while fuchsias in tubs carry the brilliant colors into the garden

ONE OF THE great things about growing plants in containers is that you can meet a particular plant's soil requirements more easily than in the garden. Such a requirement might be for neutral to acid soil, as is the case with rhododendrons and most heathers, and this is easily met by using the specially prepared acid peat mixes that are readily available. Or you might wish to grow a tubful of fine carrots, and again this is easily catered for by using a standard peat-based potting mix with additional sand, which will encourage long roots to form.

Potting Soils

By and large, however, standard potting mixes are very good and in them most plants will thrive. Apart from the standard commercial brands, there are also several potting soil packs obtainable in kit form. These supply the chemicals to which you add peat. The self-mix soils are satisfactory but they do require a large mixing area. If you use the patio floor for this purpose lay a large sheet of plastic down first to avoid making spade marks on the paving.

Of the ready mixed brands, the soil-based mixes are fine if they are correctly made with good loam, but often it is far wiser to use a peat-based mix for most plants. Home-made mixes of garden soil, peat and sand may be all right for a short while but, unless you have facilities to pasteurise the soil, you run the risk of introducing soil-borne pests and diseases.

The peat-based mixes are light in weight and this can be a disadvantage in very windy conditions, but it is better to secure the container, if necessary, than to use an inferior, though heavier, soil-based mix. Weight may also be added by including heavy drainage rocks in the base of the container. Indeed, before filling containers, it is recommended that some drainage material is added, and in large containers a layer 2 inches or so thick should be provided. Suitable drainage material can be made from pieces of broken clay pots. Broken bricks and mortar are also good but may be a bit limy for plants such as rhododendrons. Sharp-edged grit chippings are a third alternative and well cleaned stones may be better than nothing. Drainage may also be improved throughout the mix by the addition of about 10 per cent by volume of coarse sand. For plastic containers up to about 12in in size, which have plenty of drainage holes, it is not usual to add any drainage material.

Planting

Whatever mix you choose, do observe certain points before planting. First, make sure that the potting soil is moist and friable — that is crumbly — and not compacted or waterlogged, or dry as dust. If necessary, water dry soil at least a day before use to make sure that the peat has had time to absorb the moisture. Planting into dry peat mix, and then watering heavily in an attempt to get it moist, is not accepted by most plants.

Fill your chosen container with the soil to the depth necessary to take the new plant so that the top surface of the old soil is just below the top of the new container. Fill in around the rootball and to the top of the container with new potting mix

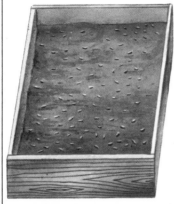

Above When starting plants from seed water after sowing and cover each flat with paper. Prick out the seedlings into 3in pots when they show secondary leaves

and water the plant in. The medium will sink to leave enough space for further watering and the plant should be at the same depth to which it was previously planted. If necessary a little more mix can be added and watered down to get the level right. It is rarely necessary to firm the mix heavily and indeed such firming may well damage roots, particularly the roots of seedlings. In a windy spot, however, some firming may be needed as well as staking. It is surprising how easily a tall leafy plant can behave like a sailing ship before the wind. If stakes are used, they should be inserted before firming or watering to settle the soil.

If you have left spaces in the patio floor for plants, plant them up in exactly the same way. If the patio has been well laid, there will be layers of sand and hardcore under the soil. The space will, therefore, be very well drained, so do make sure that there is sufficient mix or soil to support the types of plant which you intend to grow.

When planting in the ground, some firming will be necessary to steady the plant until it has got a good root hold of its own into the surrounding soil. This is particularly important with leafy plants, such as shrubs, which might otherwise become loosened by the wind. It is now considered that some back and forth movement is a good thing, helping to stimulate the plant into sending down anchor roots, but this does not mean that the plant should not be given some help. Indeed, besides light firming, in windy situations it may be necessary to add a stake. If so, put the stake in position before planting. Make sure that the planting hole is about twice as deep and wide as is actually needed to hold the rootball, fork the hole over and replace soil to bring the top of the rootball level with the surface. The backfill soil may be mixed with well rotted organic amendment, peat or used growing bag soil to improve the texture. Then fill in all round the rootball, firm lightly, and water the plant in unless the ground is already very wet and heavy. Tie the plant to a stake if one is used.

Planting against a wall is done in exactly the same way except that allowance has to be made for the fact that brick walls act like wicks and absorb moisture from the soil and this may deprive the plant. Eaves or overhanging window ledges will also probably keep some rain off the area and so shrubs and trees should be planted at least 12in away from the wall. Before planting, place any support, such as a trellis or wires, in position.

Propagating Plants

In the descriptive plant list beginning on page 40, an indication is given of the best way of reproducing each plant, whether this is by seed or other means. Many trees and shrubs take a lot of care, time and patience to raise from seed, and this also applies to certain perennial plants.

So, unless you can obtain cuttings or divisions, it is best to buy rooted container grown plants.

Increasing bulbs from offsets may not be a very practical method for the patio owner either, because the offsets must be planted somewhere to grow on until they reach flowering size, which may take a couple of years.

Annuals and biennials are easily raised from seed, and included in this category are most vegetables and herbs. Some herbs, such as rosemary or thyme, are shrubby and best bought as plants.

Sowing seed

Raising half-hardy annuals from seed means that they have to be started off indoors. Most window sills will provide ideal conditions, particularly a not too sunny one with a radiator below, because the seed is sown when the weather may be rather cold. Sow in pots or flats of seed sowing mix following the directions on the packet as far as possible with regard to depth and time of sowing. Water the seeds in and cover the container with a clear plastic bag or cling film. If using the latter, do remember to cut a small cross in the film above the seedlings when they emerge, for them to grow through; for this reason, it is a better method to use with individually sown seeds rather than those that are broadcast.

Hardy annuals are treated in the same way or may be sown directly outside when the weather has begun to warm up in mid to late spring, some varieties may also be sown in the fall.

When the seedlings are large enough they should be separated out very carefully, if they are close together, and planted up into a general potting mix either in individual pots or several to a

flat, or plastic tray.

Any plants raised indoors will need acclimating before being planted outside. This means getting them gradually accustomed to lower temperatures, perhaps by placing the pots or flats on cooler but frost-free window sills, then taking them outside on sunny frost-free days but bringing them under cover at night, until they are ready for planting out in late Spring when danger of frost is past.

Bought in seedlings and nursery stock should have a period of acclimation before sale. However, you may not be able to buy a particular named variety and, in the case of vegetables, you might not even know the name of the variety on offer. Bought plants are, therefore, very convenient but of limited choice.

Watering and Fertilizing

Container-grown plants rely entirely on the owner for their needs, except perhaps in very wet weather. How often they will need watering depends on the weather, the type and quantity of the soil, and the nature of the plant. However, all plants need adequate moisture and the aim should be to keep the soil just moist unless other instructions are given. Too much water can be dangerous, drowning the roots and killing the plant, but do remember that containers and borders close to walls dry out rapidly in warm weather.

Similarly fertilizer is needed, and particularly in periods of rapid growth, but again it is better to give too little than too much, for too much may damage the plant. There are many excellent liquid fertilizers on the market, sold either as salts to dilute or liquids to dilute.

Below Clay pots, especially those standing on sharply drained surfaces such as paving stones, lose moisture more rapidly than plastic containers, and so require careful attention

Whatever you use, follow the manufacturer's instructions with regard to dilution and rate of application. Choose a fertilizer with trace nutrients as well as the three primary plant foods — nitrogen, phosphorus and potassium, which are often abbreviated to NPK respectively.

If you cannot find a fertilizer specially formulated for pot plants, either use one where the NPK is balanced, that is it contains about the same quantities of each, or one in which the nitrogen content is less than the other two. Feeding is especially important when using soilless mixes since the materials contain no nutrients except those added; soil and soil-based mixes do have some nourishment in the loam.

General Aftercare

Permanent plants, as opposed to annuals and biennials, will need a little looking after. Trees and shrubs may need to be kept in shape by pruning or shearing individual branches in spring. Diseased or damaged wood should always be cut back to a healthy bud. Stakes and supports may need to be renewed or strengthened — a useful winter task. The base of stakes usually rots after a few years and may pull down the plant rather than support it. Check containers too, since plastic, stone and clay may split and wood rots. If a wooden container needs repainting or treating with preservative, this is also a good time for that: the plant will survive for a while perfectly happily

if well wrapped up against the weather, until the container is ready again.

Any container-grown plant is more susceptible to frost than one in the ground, since the frost can attack from all sides and especially around the root zone. This is often demonstrated by ornamentally clipped bays in small tubs, which are seen dead and shrivelled outside someone's front door after they have been left unprotected over winter. Any plant, like bay, which is not fully hardy, or you think may not be, should be protected by straw or sacking wrapped around the container to a depth of a couple of inches or more.

Tender herbaceous perennials and bulbs should also be given protection too. Bring them inside and pack them round with straw if frost threatens. At the same time, remove any dead stems and leaves.

When plants have filled their containers with roots, they may need to be taken out and divided up. This is usually done when the plants are dormant in early spring. Some plants, however, are best dealt with while they are growing, usually after flowering. Replacing old soil should be done at the same time for those plants which need fresh soil. This is only necessary every two or three years in most cases unless you are splitting up plants. Shake as much of the old soil away as possible and replace the plant in a cleaned container with new potting mix, planting as for a new plant (see page 28).

Pests and Diseases

In theory, any pest or disease with an aerial stage which attacks locally grown plants will be likely to attack your patio plants too if they are on its particular diet. Other soil pests will find the patio a convenient route to your plants. So be prepared for all the usual pests and diseases, bugs, beetles, rots and molds and, in particular, the ever present greenfly and blackfly.

In practice, if you keep the plants growing well by paying regular attention to fertilizing and watering, you should find that you do not have to deal with too many problems. Those most likely to occur are described below.

Take special care when using chemical controls if you eat out on your patio. Avoid spraying near food and tables. Also take great care if you have a patio

Below Both the nymph and adult leafhoppers take sap from plants, expel honeydew, and transmit a number of plant diseases

pond with fish in it as many garden chemicals are extremely toxic to fish.

Some of the recommended chemicals may be available in combinations with others and there should be no reason why you cannot use them provided the other chemicals are not liable to harm the particular plants you are spraying. Make sure, as well, that the recommended chemical does not carry a warning against using it on the plant you wish to treat. Do read the labels very carefully and use the chemicals in accordance with the manufacturers' instructions. All garden chemicals should be kept safely away from children and pets.

Pests

ANTS There are several species of ant which can be troublesome if you use your patio for eating out. Treat lawn areas with wormkiller and destroy aphids.

APHIDS These include greenfly — which may in fact be more pinkish, gray or yellow — as well as blackfly. They breed very rapidly and may quickly smother the stems and young parts of a plant. As they feed by sucking out the plant's sap they do the plant no good at all and, in fact, may spread virus diseases as well. Destroy as quickly as possible by picking off a small infestation or spraying with pyrethrins, or resmethrin.

BUGS Several species of bug feed on the flowers, fruits and leaves of many ornamental plants and vegetables causing distorted growth. Spray before and after flowering with malathion or carbaryl.

CATERPILLARS Fortunately there is a good array of chemicals with which to attack the many types of butterfly and moth caterpillar which may be taking meals off your plants. A good bird population will destroy many that eat the stems, leaves and flowers but this is an unreliable method and root eating caterpillars seem to have few garden enemies. Other caterpillars attack at ground level, causing plants to fall over, and these are called cutworms. Spray affected leaves, stems, flowers and fruit with malathion, carbaryl, acephate, or treat with *Bacillus thuringiensis*. Repeat the spraying as necessary and take any precautions needed, according to the manufacturers' instructions, with regard to food crops. For root caterpillars and

cutworms, apply a soil treatment of pesticide containing diazinon. Repeat if needed.

CUTWORM See Caterpillars.

EARWIGS These pests attack leaves and flowers and it is particularly annoying when you find the petals of prize blooms eaten away. Many may be caught in a small pot partially filled with straw and placed upsidedown on the end of a short cane driven into the soil. Chemically they may be discouraged by dusting with carbaryl.

LEAFHOPPERS There are several species of these very small but rather elegant looking insects. They have long bodies and legs and look rather like miniature yellowish or greenish water skaters. They eat away at leaf surfaces leaving speckled whitish marks. Some are fond of rose leaves while others are addicted to rhododendrons, but many ornamental plants may suffer. Control with malathion, diazinon, or acephate.

LEAFMINERS These grubs are undercover agents, eating away between the upper and lower leaf surfaces, leaving clearly visible whitish trails. There are several species which tunnel away in the leaves of various plants, one species being particularly attracted to chrysanthemums. Spray affected plants with acephate on non-edible crops, or diazinon on food crops, if squashing the individual grubs, enclosed between the leaf surfaces, does not appeal to you.

MEALY BUGS This aphid type of insect hides under a coat of a whitish, waxy material. It may be found on newly bought plants or those brought outside from greenhouses, as well as on fruit trees. Soak with a malathion spray.

MITES These are very tiny insects, usually seen on the undersides of leaves. They spin a fine spidery web to live in but are, in fact, mites which suck the plant juices. Affected leaves take on a sickly, mottled appearance and often become darkened with blackish mold. They are most likely to be found on plants brought out from the greenhouse, and should be treated with dicofol, or acephate or malathion.

ROOT FLIES Various flies may attack flower and vegetable roots. The flies lay

Above Aphids are soft bodied, sucking insects which secrete honeydew, that in turn attracts ants and sooty mold

Below Leafminers make blisters and snaking tunnels in the leaves of many plants such as holly, lilac, blackberry, peas, raspberry and chrysanthemums. They also disfigure the fruit of apple

33

Above Mites cause bronzing and shrivelling of leaves, and may completely defoliate a plant

Below Thrips scar fruit and foliage, though some types prey on harmful mites and other small insects

the eggs, their grubs do the damage. The whitish grubs or maggots eat away and tunnel into the roots or bulbs. Plants may die. Attacked leaves of cabbage family plants, including wallflowers, honesty and many vegetables, turn bluish before the plants die. Carrot leaves turn yellow and orange. Treat soil with insecticide containing diazinon before planting. In the case of established plants, treat the soil in spring, gently hand forking similar insecticide into the soil around the plants.

SCALE INSECTS These are small creatures which are pressed flat to the stems or leaves of infected plants, their bodies covered by a scale-like upper cover and often rather waxy. Plants may become severely infested by one or more of the different species. The different species vary in shape. One shape may give rise to the common name mussel scale for those resembling minute mussels. Other species may be round and humped. Treat with malathion; several repeat applications may be required.

SLUGS AND SNAILS If you have anything tender growing on your patio or anything tender in a windowbox within reach, you may be sure that slugs or snails, or both, will make a meal from them. These pests usually munch away in the darker hours, leaving a ragged mess of partially chewed leaves. Treat the soil around plants with liberal quantities of methiocarb granules or metaldehyde formulation. Repeat dressings will certainly be necessary.

THRIPS These tiny black insects resemble printed hyphens and cluster in flowers. Their rasping away gives the petals a blotchy appearance. Treat affected flowers with insecticides containing acephate, or diazinon, or malathion.

VINE WEEVIL Brown-headed white-bodied soil pests, rather like large fly grubs, these creatures eat the roots of many ornamental plants, including tubers and corms. Unfortunately the first sign of attack may be the collapse of the plant. The adult weevils, deep brownish black little beetles, attack the leaves of a number of plants, including rhododendrons and primulas, creating ragged holes around the leaf edges. Treat both with insecticide containing diazinon.

WHITEFLY These small white flies take

to the wing when affected plants are disturbed. These pests feed and breed continuously in warm conditions, weakening plants. Sticky honeydew is produced, often followed by black molds, which disfigure leaves and stems as well as growing points.

Spray affected plants with insecticide containing malathion or resmethrin every seven days while the trouble continues.

WOODLICE Apparently unassuming little insects, woodlice quietly go about their business eating roots and stems, particularly those already damaged by some other pest. Grayish when adult, the young are pink and similarly covered by a series of overlapping scales. Treat with methiocarb.

Diseases and disorders

BLACKSPOT A great nuisance on roses, blackspot not only needs chemical control but strict hygiene as well. Blackish spots appear on the leaves and spread, the leaves then yellow and fall and the stems begin dying back. Any fallen leaves and prunings of diseased plants should be gathered up and burned. The blackspot fungus can overwinter on such debris to reinfect plants the next year if not destroyed. Spray affected plants and surrounding soil with benomyl or triforine.

BOTRYTIS This disease is also descriptively called grey mold, affected plants becoming covered with a mold which causes rapid rotting. Strawberries, clarkias, dahlias, godetias, lilies, peonies, petunias, roses, zinnias, courgettes and lettuces are also particularly liable to be attacked and especially in wet weather. Remove the diseased plants or affected parts, and spray the remaining plant or plants with benomyl, maneb or mancozeb.

CHLOROSIS A disorder due to some deficiency, the usual problem being lack of iron available to the plant in alkaline soil or potting mix. Azaleas and rhododendrons are commonly affected. Other plants, such as camellias, ceanothus and hydrangeas, may also develop the typical symptoms with leaves yellowing between the veins. Make sure that such plants are growing in a good potting soil or soil mix and for the plants concerned a special rhododendron acid soil mix is available. Treat affected plants with sulfate of iron with added trace elements, and always water them if you can with soft water — rain water rather than tap.

DAMPING OFF Typical signs of this trouble are collapse and death of seedlings, often followed by white or pinkish molds. Prevention is the best course of action. Use clean containers and a seed mix.

Don't waterlog seeds or seedlings and avoid excessive temperatures.

DOWNY MILDEW This may not be recognised at first as usually the upper surfaces of leaves develop dull or yellowish patches while the grayish mildew develops on the under surfaces. Snapdragons, sweet peas, lettuces and wallflowers are among plants which may be affected, particularly in damp weather. Spray with zineb, benomyl or dinocap.

GREY MOLD See Botrytis.

LEAF SPOTS There are a number of fungal diseases which cause flat leaf spots, or blotches, of various sizes and colors (blackspot has been described earlier). See also Rusts and Viruses. Many plants may be affected. Sprays may help but are not always successful. Try fungicide sprays containing benomyl, copper, mancozeb, or maneb.

MILDEWS AND MOLDS See Botrytis, Downy mildew and Powdery mildew.

POWDERY MILDEW The gray powdery appearance of the leaves, shoots, buds or flowers of affected plants makes this disease unmistakeable. It often appears in hot, dry weather. A whole range of plants may become affected including begonias, chrysanthemums, delphiniums, michaelmas daisies and roses. Spray with benomyl, dinocap or triflorine on ornamental plants only, maneb also for roses. In the fall, cut out and burn affected branches of shrubs and trees.

RUSTS The leaf spots of rust infections have a raised powdery surface, often of an orange color, but possibly yellow or brownish. See also Leaf spots and Viruses. Many plants, including carnations, chrysanthemums, fuchsias, hollyhocks, mint, geraniums, roses and sweet williams, may be affected, sometimes seriously. Spray affected plants with fungicide containing maneb, folpet, triforine or zineb on ornamental plants only.

VIRUSES Virus diseases may seriously distort plant growth or appear as blotches, streaks or mottling on leaves or flowers. Viruses are generally spread by insects, your own hands from touching infected material or, similarly, by gardening tools. Camellias, chrysanthemums, courgettes, daffodils, dahlias, lettuces, lilies, geraniums, strawberries, sweet peas and tomatoes are among the plants likely to be affected. Unfortunately there is no known cure and affected plants should be dug up and burnt.

WILTS Several fungi may cause plants to collapse suddenly, leaves and stems wilting and looking as though the plant is completely dead. Clematis are particularly affected. Cut back the wilted part as many plants will regrow. Spray the new growth with fungicide containing benomyl or copper and also soak the surrounding soil with the chosen chemical.

Above Blackspot is usually worse in warm wet seasons. The disease is usually controlled by picking off and burning the affected leaves

Below Chlorosis could be the result of one of a number of physiological disorders. It is commonly rectified by giving plants a balanced diet, and additional iron

CHAPTER FOUR

COLOR THE YEAR ROUND

Opposite Lush hostas, scarlet and pink impatiens, and hederas and cotoneasters drape down patio steps in a profusion of different forms and colors. Even when the fuchsias, potted geraniums and sweet alyssums have finished flowering this planting scheme will hold interest throughout the year

Below A raised wooden crate bed with spring flowers, narcissus, tulips and grape hyacinths providing an eye-catching focal point under a rustic pergola

WHAT PLANTS YOU grow is such a matter of personal choice that no fixed rules can be laid down. Some people are content with just a blaze of color through the summer but little for the rest of the year. And planting schemes chosen from the range of brilliant annuals and bedding plants will give just that. Other people prefer a quieter but longer lasting display, using bulbs, perennial plants, shrubs and conifers. And again the choice of plants is very wide indeed. Here are a few ideas that may help you make the best display from your choice of plants.

The use of foliage plants to provide a background to other lower growing flowering plants will help to show off the blooms, especially if it is the dark foliage of many conifers. Such plants may also make a permanent backbone to your scheme, as will other evergreens or deciduous trees or shrubs.

Evergreens with dark or light green, yellow or variegated foliage will supply color through the year. They will also make an attractive edging or hedging around a patio.

It is almost possible to have flowers in bloom throughout the year too, but this requires either a great deal of space in order to grow a wide enough range of plants or a constant change of plant. For instance, crocus species and varieties may be grown to flower from September to May but obviously to get a worthwhile show you will need quite a few different species and varieties and quite a number of bulbs of each. Even then, all your efforts may be fouled up by the weather, which may delay or hasten flowering.

Color Schemes

When you are considering what colors go together, generally hot colors do not mix well with pastel colors. For example, fiery scarlet salvias do not look at all well with pink spider flower but will make a startlingly strong, yet interesting contrast when grown with deep blue lobelias or convolvulus. The spider flower will, however, blend in with the lilac-blue periwinkle, *Vinca minor*. In fact, most pinks will go well with lilac and lavender shades, and buff and lemon yellows will go with both hot and pastel color schemes.

White is often a good barrier between other colors. Sweet alyssum (*Lobularia*) is often used as a buffer between scarlet salvia and blue lobelia in bedding schemes. Gray and silver foliage, as found in some English ivies and *Centaurea gymnocarpa*, will perform the same function.

Planting Arrangements

Two simple but effective planting schemes have already been mentioned under hanging baskets (page 27), and, generally speaking, the fewer the different types of plant involved, the most pleasing the planting will appear. Windowboxes and hanging baskets are all too often overcrowded with lots of different plants, when it would be more effective to use a number of plants of fewer varieties, a point which applies to all small planting schemes, and in particular all containers. For example, a blue-green conifer, such as the Chinese juniper 'Obelisk', is a superb sight set round with crimson daisies (*Bellis*) and needs no other plants to distract the eye. The juniper provides all year round interest with the daisies adding color in spring and summer. The juniper, however, is only useful in windowboxes and hanging baskets while it is young and not too tall, after a few years it will probably have to continue life in a ground-based container.

Another very simple, yet charming color scheme, is provided by evergreen, silver-leaved and pink-flowered pinks (*Dianthus*) making a permanent center to annually planted deep blue lobelia, particularly if a trailing lobelia is chosen.

More ambitious perhaps, using three different plants for a bolder effect, would be a purple and red flowered fuchsia — two or three or more plants may be required depending on the size of your windowbox, basket or other container — surrounded by the dwarf variegated grass, *Holcus mollis* 'Albovariegatus', the edges being furnished by the trailing, scented *Thunbergia fragrans* 'Angel Wings', with yellow-eyed white flowers. The thunbergia is the only annual in this scheme and it can be planted in early summer over permanent spring-flowered bulbs, such as scillas or muscari, which also die down early and will not clash with the fuchsia flowers. These small bulbs, and snowdrops and hyacinths, are among the best for early color as they are permanent residents of the container.

More spectacular, but requiring planting each year, are the cinerarias (*Senecio* x *hybridus*) with their large heads of bright daisy flowers in blues and reds and pinks and white. They are at their best in towns, set against the gray buildings, where they may provide a bit of color between dwarf conifers.

Most of the colorful plants are at their best from late spring to fall and there is less color later in the year. It is then that the burning bush (*Kochia*) comes into its

Right The cluster heads of verbena, the 'daisy' flowers of dimorphotheca, and most geraniums and fuchsia blooms will appear from June to the early fall. This arrangement includes senecio for its distinctive, gray fronds

Left A mixed collection of succulents in a stone trough. The sempervivums with their evergreen leaf rosettes, and the perennial saxifrages which form dense mats or hummocks, often with flowers in the spring, are ideal for long term displays

own, assuming a brilliant purplish-red foliage color after having been a bright green through the summer. It makes a good windowbox plant and looks well surrounded by dwarf geraniums (zonal pelargoniums), pink-flowered petunias or daisies.

A very interesting and useful window box may be made using annual herbs in the same way as flowering and foliage plants. Here the place of the taller burning bush or conifer is taken by, say, the sweet pepper 'Golden Bell', which fruits well out of doors. This is surrounded by sweet basil which, in turn, is outflanked, or surrounded, by the rather floppy sweet marjoram. The grayish leaves of the marjoram contrast with the bright green basil and dark leaved, but yellow fruited, pepper. They all need fairly similar conditions, sun, warmth and moisture. The pepper and basil may require short stakes for support. The bonus of having an interesting vegetable and less easily obtainable herbs makes this a very worthwhile planting scheme.

A more permanent herb windowbox might be made up from centrally planted common marjoram with clumps of chives and garden thyme surrounding it and an edging of trailing thyme. All these herbs may also be grown with flowering plants to give a greater decorative effect, the common marjoram, perhaps, surrounded by petunias, or an edging planted alternatively with sweet marjoram and trailing lobelia to combine attractiveness and usefulness.

In winter, when the riot of flowering plants is past, evergreen plants come into their own. Fortunately there is a good range to choose from and, by contrasting leaf shape as well as color, very attractive arrangements may be made in windowboxes or patio containers. Try a dwarf conifer, such as the dwarf Norway spruce, *Picea abies* 'Gregoryana', for the center height and surround it with the black-purple leaved mondo grass, and contrast those ribbon leaves with the irregularly lobed leaves of a variegated English ivy, such as *Hedera helix* 'Tricolor', which also has a pinkish tinge to blend with the dark ribbons. Alternatives might include a dwarf pine, such as *Pinus densiflora* 'Umbraculifera', surrounded simply by a variegated periwinkle (*Vinca*) which will carpet the surface and drape over the edges to provide flowers for much of the year.

CHAPTER FIVE

AN A TO Z OF ORNAMENTAL PLANTS

Opposite Abutilon 'Suntense' makes a splendid wall shrub, but needs the protection of straw or sacking at its roots in the winter months

Below Acanthus spinosus, with its tall flower spikes towering above the thistle like foliage, makes a good background plant behind ground hugging species

THERE ARE MANY plants that are well adapted for the smallest patio, and a number of plants that are not adapted for any size of patio, windowbox or hanging basket at all. The plants described in this chapter are useful for various sizes of patio and many are also good for windowboxes or hanging baskets — but not the other way round unless you have some big boxes or baskets. Even though the choice for these containers is obviously not so great there is still a wide selection of form, size and color, and, however small the amount of space you can spare for growing plants, something colorful and something attractive may be achieved with a little thought and planning.

Unless special conditions are mentioned for the plants described, plant them in fresh peat-based mix in containers.

Abutilon

DECIDUOUS SHRUBS Not fully hardy, the abutilons make splendid shrubs in pots or beds against a sunny wall. Their rapid growth makes them good plants to provide a colorful, bushy effect quickly. The hanging bell-shaped summer flowers of most are set against vine or maple like foliage.

The following varieties of *A.* x *hybridum* may reach 8ft in height, 'Ashford Red' has deep rose red flowers; 'Boule de Neige', white flowers; 'Golden Fleece', golden-yellow flowers; 'Orange Glow', orange-yellow flowers; 'Savitzii', yellow flowers on a smaller bush with white-splashed leaves. *A. megapotamicum*, to 7ft tall, red and yellow flowers; 'Variegatum', with leaves mottled

yellow. *A.* x *suntense*, to 10ft tall, has more open, lilac-lavender flowers.

Repot in spring and cut the plants hard back then. Increase by cuttings in spring. Zones 9–10.

Acantholimon

ROCK PLANTS These spiny, thrift-like perennial plants form evergreen cushions and are excellent for sunny walls or very well drained holes in the patio floor. They are sometimes known as prickly thrifts or prickly heaths and have mainly pink flowers carried in small spikes. They grow slowly to about 6in tall with a spread about twice that.

Acantholimon echinus (A. androsaceum) has pink to reddish flowers over bluish-green leaves. *A. glumaceum*, pink flowers, deep green leaves. *A. olivieri*, rose-pink flowers, gray-green leaves.

To increase, divide plants in early fall. Zone 8.

Acanthus

HARDY HERBACEOUS PERENNIALS Imposing deciduous plants, known as bear's breeches, which will make spectacular specimens, either set into the floor of the patio or in a suitable large container, in a sunny site. Magnificent large, deeply cut leaves form a rosette from which grows a tall spike of flowers.

The best kinds are *A. longifolius*, 2½–3ft tall, flowers rosy violet. *A. mollis*, 3–4ft tall, flowers whitish to purplish pink. *A. m.* 'Latifolius', 3½ft tall, flowers lilac rose. *A. spinosus*, 3–6½ft tall, flowers white to purple, leaves deep green, makes a good specimen plant.

Increase by division in spring or fall or by sowing seed. Zones 8–9.

Acer

DECIDUOUS TREES AND SHRUBS Superbly colored foliage makes some of the deciduous maples ideal for a patio, as very ornamental specimens or background plants. Grow either in a patio paving space or in a suitable large container in good soil and sheltered position.

Acer circinatum, the vine maple, usually bushy but may grow into a small tree, has lobed, roundish leaves which turn vivid red and orange in the fall. *Acer palmatum* has a number of low-growing and slow-growing varieties, generally a few metres high they include 'Atropurpureum', leaves bronze red to crimson all summer; 'Aureum', leaves yellow; 'Corallinum', young stems and leaves pink; 'Dissectum Atropurpureum', leaves purple red; 'Dissectum Flavescens', young leaves yellow green.

No regular pruning required. Increase by ripe seed and by grafting. Zones 5–9.

Aethionema

ROCK PLANTS Suitable for well drained sites, such as cracks in patio paving, the stone cresses make small shrubby or perennial mounds. They are evergreen. And make an eyecatching show, for weeks on end, when covered with long lasting clear pink flowers in early

summer. *A. grandiflorum*, Persian stone cress, to 12in in height and with a similar spread, flowers rose-pink. *A.* 'Warley Rose', a compact hybrid, to about 6in but spreads to twice that, brilliant rose-pink flowers.

Increase by summer cuttings, seed sown in spring also for the Persian stone cress. Zones 6–9.

Agapanthus

HERBACEOUS PERENNIALS The African lilies are superb, deciduous perennials that make excellent container plants and also do well in a patio paving space. They have strap-shaped leaves and large balls of blue or white flowers on tall stems in summer. Preferring sun, they will also do quite well in partial shade.

There is a splendid hardy group of plants derived from various species and known as 'Headbourne Hybrids'. These are available with flowers ranging from deep blue to a very pale blue and white, and varying in height from 2–4ft.

Increase by division of the fleshy roots or seed sown in spring; seed-raised plants will vary in color. Zones 9–10.

Ageratum

HALF-HARDY ANNUALS Ageratum is excellent as a quick color filler for odd spots on a patio or as ground cover in containers, including windowboxes and hanging baskets. It prefers sun.

Many strains of *A. houstonianum* are

available and are constantly being added to by the plant breeders. Flowers vary from deep lilac through pink to white, and the plants grow 5–24in according to variety.

Raise annually from seed sown indoors in spring. Zones 5–10.

Ajuga

HARDY HERBACEOUS PERENNIALS
Bugles make excellent dwarf plants for shady parts of a patio or windowbox and make good ground cover under other plants. They need to be kept moist. All spread, some rapidly, and this should be borne in mind when consideration is given to planting them in a container or patio. A number have attractively colored leaves.

Ajuga genevensis has bright blue, pink or white flowers and grows 6–12in tall. *A. pyramidalis* has blue and purple flowers 9in tall; it has a form 'Crispa' (*A. metallica crispa*) with wrinkled dark metallic leaves but it often dies out rather quickly. *A. reptans*, the common bugle, is a rapid spreader and good if that is required, flowers in shades of violet, pink or white, 4–12in; it has various forms with colored leaves, such as 'Burgundy Glow', leaves purple, reddish and gold; 'Multicolor' ('Rainbow'), leaves green, bronze, gold and pink.

Increase by seed or division in spring. Zones 2–3.

Alchemilla

HARDY HERBACEOUS PERENNIALS
Grown as foliage plants, lady's mantles are tolerant of most soils and add a quiet note to other planting schemes, blending and softening harsher colours and contours. They are low growing with round or lobed leaves and do well in sun or shade. The flowers are minute and yellow green.

Alchemilla alpina, alpine lady's mantle, good for a cool spot in paving crevices, green leaves silvery below, grows about 6in tall. *A. erythropoda*, is similar but with gray-green leaves. *A. hookerii* forms a silvery mound. *A. mollis*, common lady's mantle, has bluish-green leaves and is taller growing, 12–18in, and may spread very rapidly by self-sown seed.

Increase by division or seed sown in spring. Zone 3.

Above Salmon, pink and maroon hollyhocks planted against a sunny wall on the patio are excellent for providing color above ground level. Here they hide the low, bare stems of *Clematis jackmanii*

Althaea

HARDY HERBACEOUS PERENNIALS
With their backs against a sunny house wall, hollyhocks give a patio a breath of life and yet a cottagey charm. They are deciduous perennials, seldom long lived and often grown as annuals or biennials. If there is no planting space left between wall and patio, use large containers and enrich the soil with organic amendment to get the tallest plants.

There are many strains of *A. rosea*, probably hybrids with *A. ficifolia*, offered in seedsmen's catalogues; they come in a wide range of flower color, from near black to crimson, red, shades of pink and carmine, orange, yellow or white, and in single or double forms. Height varies according to strain and conditions, 2–8ft.

Increase by seed sown in spring. Zones 2–3.

Alyssum (Aurinia)

HARDY HERBACEOUS PERENNIALS
Alyssums are usually golden flowered perennials or shrubby plants but the name is often used for a dwarf bedding plant called *Lobularia* with white or pinkish flowers. The true alyssums form clumps, are very hardy but prefer a sunny spot. Plant in cracks or containers filled with well draining soil.

Above A carpet of *Anagallis phillipsii* will greatly enhance a patio flower bed. There are a number of species of *Anagalus,* some of which are perennial, but all are treated as annuals in cultivation

Alyssum montanum has scented yellow flowers, grayish leaves and is mat forming, up to 6in. *A. saxatile*, gold dust, has spring flowers in various shades of yellow, such as 'Citrinum', lemon yellow, or 'Dudley Neville', buff yellow with gray-green leaves.

Increase by seed sown in spring or cuttings in early fall. Zones 2–3.

Anagallis

HALF-HARDY ANNUALS   These brightly flowered, dwarf, spreading pimpernels add a terrific splash of color all summer. Good as a carpet beneath other plants provided that they are not in shade, they will enliven the surroundings of such permanent plants as dwarf conifers, in tubs or windowboxes.

Mixed seed of *A. linifolia (A. monellii)* provides a sheet of flowers in shades of red, pink and gentian blue, and grows about 6in.

Raise annually from seed sown in spring indoors. Zones 3–8.

Androsace

ROCK PLANTS   The rock jasmines are excellent plants for filling in cracks or crevices in a patio floor or wall, or in troughs, in a sunny position. The soil should be rich in humus but well draining. These small plants are hardy but require some care.

Androsace chamaejasme forms mats of hairy leaves 1–2in high, above which perch, in late spring to the end of summer, whitish flowers that turn pink. *A. lanuginosa*, has pink flowers from summer to fall above silver mats of trailing leaves. *A. primuloides (A. sarmentosa)* has a number of strains including 'Chumbyi', with large pink flowers over very silvery leaves, about 3in tall.

Increase by division after flowering or by seed. Zones 5–6.

Anemone

HARDY HERBACEOUS PERENNIALS There are many deciduous anemones to choose from, some ideal for window boxes or growing in other containers. Their characteristics are diverse and described separately under each plant named below.

Anemone apennina, grows from a tuberous rhizome and has blue, white or pink flowers in spring; for cool, partial shade, in well drained conditions, in tubs, windowboxes or holes in the patio; to 8in tall. *A. blanda* is similar but with flowers of pink, purple, blue, white or red and grows to about 6in, the variety 'Atrocoerulea' has deep blue flowers; 'Radar' has white-centred red flowers.

Anemone coronaria, very colorful in windowboxes, has two main popular forms with large, brightly colored summer flowers, 'De Caen' being single flowered and 'St Brigid' semi-double. They grow from tubers and are 6–12in tall. *A.* x *hybridus*, the garden Japanese anemone, often sold under other names, such as *A. japonica* and *A. elegans*, is an herbaceous perennial with flowers of pink to purple or white in late summer; it grows 3–5ft tall and is good for beds around the patio, as an accent clump in a patio floor space or in large containers.

Increase by division in fall or by seed sown in late spring or root cuttings in spring. Zones 5–8.

Anthemis

HARDY HERBACEOUS PERENNIALS Mat or clump forming perennials with yellow or white daisy flowers over finely divided foliage. Grow in a sunny spot and, according to size of plant, in a suitable container. Or in the case of chamomile, as a non-flowering lawn.

Anthemis cupaniana is splendid for covering a patio space, growing only about 6–10in high but 3ft wide, the silvery gray, aromatic, evergreen foliage dotted with large white daisies from spring to fall. *A. tinctoria* and *A. sanctijohannis* have produced several good, deciduous, yellow, summer-flowering hybrids which grow up to about 2½ft, 'E. C. Buxton' has lemon-yellow flowers; 'Grallagh Gold', bright yellow; both good in a raised bed, patio, paving space or in larger containers.

Increase by division or cuttings in summer. Zones 3–5.

Antirrhinum

GROWN AS HALF-HARDY ANNUALS The snapdragons make a very colorful display and the modern strains accept most containers. Though perennial they are grown as annuals. The dwarf types are excellent in windowboxes or small containers, but grow them all in a sunny spot.

Antirrhinum majus, common snapdragon, has strains of various mixed colors as well as single color varieties, and they include 'Cheerio', large, colorful flowers in mixed colors, 18in; 'Minaret', early and wide color range, 15–18in; 'Double Madame Butterfly', large, double flowers rather like azaleas, wide color range, 2–2½ft; 'Pixie', many colors, only 10in tall and 'Little Gem', mixed, small flowers in a good range of color, 4–6in. Single colors available include 'Black Prince', deep crimson, bronze leaves, 18in; 'Dazzler', vermilion, 18in; 'Coral Monarch', deep rose with buff, 18in; 'Yellow Monarch', clear yellow, 18in.

Sow under glass in spring in unsterilized mix, or in the open in the fall. Zones 5–10.

Arabis

HARDY HERBACEOUS PERENNIALS Excellent, low-growing, evergreen plants, the rock cresses are good in cracks in a patio wall or paving and in sun. They are also good trailing from hanging baskets and windowboxes.

Arabis blepharophylla has strains with flowers mainly in shades of pink or white over neat-growing tufts of stiff leaves,

4–6in. *A. caerulea*, lilac-blue flowers over small tufts of foliage, 4in, will grow in small pockets of peaty soil or mix. *A. caucasica (A. albida)*, the common white rock cress is very invasive unless confined by a suitably inhospitable wall or other setting, mats of gray leaves, to 10cm; it has a few compact varieties or hybrids, 'Rosabella' with rosy flowers, 'Flore Pleno' with double white flowers, and 'Variegata' with yellow and white variegated leaves. *A. ferdinandii-coburgii*, white flowers over compact gray leaves but best known for its variety 'Variegata', a good variegated plant with white and green leaves.

Increase by cuttings in summer, division in the fall or sow seed in spring. Zones 6, 7.

Armeria

HARDY HERBACEOUS PERENNIALS Thrift is a splendid, evergreen crack filler in well draining patios. It forms mounds of leaves above which the flowers appear in profusion in early summer and it does well in sun and partial shade.

Armeria juniperifolia (A. caespitosa), a dwarf thrift, carries its pink flowers just above the foliage, 2–4in high and good on walls. *A. maritima*, sea pink, sea thrift, with pink flowers above a dark green cushion of leaves, 4–12in high, has several varieties with flowers deep pink to white.

Increase by division or seed sown in spring, or cuttings in summer. Zone 3.

Above The fragrant flowers of antirrhinum (snapdragon) sown in mixed colors make a lively display edging a patio border or filling small containers

Below Arabis rosea transforms a dry stone wall with a mound of mauve, rounded petals. Some arabis species are so invasive they are regarded as weeds

Asplenium

HARDY FERNS The spleenworts are fine evergreen ferns for growing in walls or in such places as the corners of patio steps. Use a gritty soil and plant in a light but not necessarily a sunny spot.

Asplenium adiantum-nigrum, black spleenwort, has black stalked fronds 4–14in long. *A. scolopendrium (Phyllitis)*, hart's tongue fern, has tongue- or strap-shaped fronds, usually without leaflets though often wavy edged, (8–24in) long. *A. s.* 'Cristatum', has unusual tasseled fronds. *A. trichomanes*, maidenhair spleenwort, has dark red stalks, round leaflets and fronds 2–10in long.

Increase by division in spring. Zone 3.

Astilbe

HARDY HERBACEOUS PERENNIALS Much favored for their plumes of red, pink or white, feathery flowers, astilbes thrive in many conditions and are suitable for most uses. Specimen clumps in a patio paving space or raised bed make a quietly attractive feature.

There are many good hybrids and species, a few of which are mentioned here. *A.* x *arendsii* hybrids, 'Amethyst', lilac-pink, to 3ft; 'Deutschland', white, 2ft; 'Fanal', garnet red, 2ft. *A.* x *crispa* hybrids, 'Perkeo', pink, 10in; 'Peter Pan', deep pink, 10in. *A. simplicifolia* hybrids, 'Altro-rosea', large heads of intense pink, 14in; 'Bronze Elegance', rose, bronzy foliage, 10–12in, best in light shade; 'Nana', pink, 6in.

Increase by division in spring or fall. Zone 6.

Athyrium

HARDY FERNS Excellent for moist positions, providing deciduous greenery in shady patio corners, window boxes or hanging baskets. *A. filix-femina*, the lady fern, has many varieties including *cristatum* with flatly crested fronds, 2–2½ft; 'Minutum', dwarf at about 6in; 'Victoriae' lattice work fronds, 3ft, *plumosum*, feathery fronds, 2½ft. *A. goeringianum*, has drooping fronds with purplish stalks, 8–18in, and in its variety 'Pictum' the gray leaves are on dark red stalks.

Increase by division in spring or fall. Zone 3.

Aubrieta

HARDY HERBACEOUS PERENNIALS Colorful patio plants, excellent for a sunny position where they may be allowed to sprawl; very good on walls or tumbling down steps. Aubrietas are suitable for most soils or potting mixes preferably lime rich.

There are many hybrids derived from *A. deltoidea*. These form mats, 4–8in high, of usually grayish to green leaves, though some have variegated foliage. They flower in spring and early summer. Varieties include 'Argenteovariegata' ('Variegata'), lilac flowers, leaves variegated white; 'Aureovariegata' ('Aurea'), lavender flowers, leaves variegated yellow; 'Bob Saunders', double reddish-purple flowers; 'Bressingham Pink', double pink; 'Dr Mules', violet.

Increase by division in the fall. Zone 4.

Begonia

TENDER HERBACEOUS PERENNIALS There are three main types of begonia dealt with here, and all are very good in their different ways. They are the popular fibrous-rooted begonias used so often in mass summer schemes, the tuberous begonias, including the pendulous types, and the begonias grown as foliage plants. These different begonias will fill many patio, windowbox and hanging basket needs. Zone 10

Begonia rex provides many varieties with colored leaves, often marbled or splashed with pinks, reds, crimson, bronze and almost black. Keep moist when planted in containers including

Below Particularly effective planted around a pool *Astilbe arendsii* 'Fanal' carries minute deep red flowers in long panicles. This plant looks well with irises

hanging baskets and windowboxes. It is tender and can only be used outdoors in the summer. Increase by leaf cuttings.

Begonia semperflorens, the wax begonia, is fibrous rooted and may be used for a wide variety of purposes including windowboxes, hanging baskets, cracks in patio paving or for filling urns and other containers as well as any patio beds. Easy to grow, it appreciates sun and some moisture. Many varieties and colorful mixtures are listed, some with bronze or chocolate leaves, including 'Organdy', flowers in pink and red shades and white, green, purple and bronze leaves, 4–12in. Easily raised from seed, the plants may be grown on through the winter indoors.

Begonia x *tuberhybrida* is a name covering a range of tuberous-rooted hybrids with various characteristics. All have brilliant flowers, the colors ranging from crimson, through red and orange to pinks, yellows and white; some have petals edged in another color. Most make compact, bushy plants and usually have strong green foliage. They are good in most sunny positions and often do very well in light shade, but keep them moist while growing. In early spring the tubers are potted up and grown on indoors until early summer when they can be planted out. There are many selections varying in size of flower, leaf and height and some are pendulous and so ideal for hanging baskets or trailing over windowsills. Zones 9–10.

Bellis

HARDY HERBACEOUS PERENNIALS The large-flowered forms of the English daisy make a long lasting display in spring, good for massing under taller growing plants in large containers or windowboxes, or for edging. The plants grow into thick clumps. Almost any sunny or partially shaded site and any potting mix or soil are suitable.

Bellis perennis is usually available in two forms, the very large flowered Monstrosa type and the smaller (but still much larger than the lawn daisy) Miniature. Both have pompon flowers in shades of crimson and pink as well as white. The plants are evergreen and grow to about 4–6in tall and at least as wide. They are best treated as biennials and raised afresh each year.

Increase by seed or division in spring. Zones 3–8.

Berberis

HARDY EVERGREEN AND DECIDUOUS SHRUBS The barberries provide some splendid shrubs and hedging plants as well as one or two excellent little plants for windowboxes or containers on the patio. Grow in sun or partial shade.

Berberis x *stenophylla*, 'Corallina Compacta' has rich yolk-yellow flowers, fine, pointed, evergreen leaves, and grows to about 1ft. *B. thunbergii* 'Atropurpurea Nana' has small spoon-shaped purple leaves; in *B. t.* 'Aurea' the leaves are yellowish but deepening to green as the season progresses, both are deciduous and grow to about 2ft.

Above The fibrous rooted *Begonia semperflorens* adapts to a variety of uses, but though requiring plenty of moisture always appreciates a well drained rooting medium.

Left A double form of *Bellis perennis*. These pompon daisies can be planted out in October and November in a sunny or partially shaded patch of garden soil. Alternatively, give them some protection over winter and plant out in spring

Increase by heeled cuttings from late summer to early fall. Zones 5–9.

Blechnum

HARDY FERNS These very fine evergreen plants are known as hard ferns because of their tough, leathery leaves. They grow well in shady spots but do not like lime so use a good peat-based compost, preferably neutral or one suitable for acid-loving plants.

Blechnum penna marina, dwarf hard fern, makes a creeping clump about 6in high. *B. spicant*, deer fern, has sterile fronds which lie flat, and fertile, erect fronds up to 2ft tall.

Divide in spring to increase them or reduce their spreads. Zones 4–9.

Buxus

HARDY EVERGREEN SHRUBS Boxwood is one of the most adaptable of plants. Use it as trimmed edging by all means, or for neat little bushes in patio boxes or windowboxes. Evergreen and hardy, box does well in alkaline soils or potting mix,

and in sun or light shade.

Buxus sempervirens is a slow-growing shrub, eventually reaching a height of 16–23ft but usually confined to much less by trimming. The typical boxwood has dark green leaves but there are a number of variations, some with variegated leaves, and there is also 'Suffruticosa', which is the typical edging boxwood, of dwarf habit, which may be kept down to about 6in or left to grow to 3ft or more.

Increase by late summer to early fall cuttings. Zones 6–10.

Calandrinia

GROWN AS HALF-HARDY ANNUALS Brilliant flowers of eye-catching color make this trailing plant an admirable choice for containers of all sorts, including windowboxes and hanging baskets, as well as for draping down patio steps or edges from crevices in the paving. Plants sometimes may self-seed freely in a warm sheltered environment. Though a tender perennial it is grown as a half-hardy annual. Plant in sun in well draining soil or potting mix and do not overwater.

Calandrinia umbellata, rock purslane, has startling magenta flowers, or vivid crimson in the variety 'Amaranth', set over gray-green leaves, height about 6in.

Sow seed in spring indoors. Zones 5–9.

Camellia

HARDY AND SLIGHTLY TENDER EVERGREEN SHRUBS Outstanding shrubs for a patio, camellias do well in containers for a time but are better if planted in the soil and protected by a wall, when they make a superb backdrop for a patio. Moreover they will accept quite a lot of shade if the situation is fairly open. Plant in neutral to slightly acid soil or a potting mix which has been formulated for acid loving plants. Feed with liquid fertilizer during the growing season.

Camellia japonica has a large number of varieties in pinks, carmine-reds and white, with double and single flowers of various types. *C.* x *williamsii* has similar flower forms but is considered to be rather hardier than *C. japonica*. It also has a wide array of varieties. Most will eventually reach 6½–10ft depending on situation and restriction of growth.

Increase by cuttings in early fall. Zones 7–9.

Below Native to India, China and Japan, camellias are generally hardy shrubs but need an acid soil. Besides the splendid rose sized blooms they carry dark, glossy, evergreen leaves

Campanula

HARDY HERBACEOUS PERENNIALS AND ROCK PLANTS   A number of campanulas, or bellflowers, make lovely flowering plants for patios and containers, some are good for paving cracks, others for hanging baskets or pots. Many tall kinds make good cut flowers. Try *C. isophylla* as a flowering houseplant. All have flowers in shades of violet, lavender blue or white. They appreciate an open position in sun or light shade and well draining soils and potting mixes.

Campanula persicifolia, a hardy perennial, has a number of varieties including the almost blue 'Percy Piper' with tall, 3ft, spikes of flower. It looks good as a clump-forming patio space filler or in a raised bed and does very well in large pots. *C. poscharskyana*, very hardy, is a rock plant which will succeed where others fail. Once established — in a pot, patio space, windowbox or hanging basket — it will fill every crack and crevice with self-sown seedlings. It has floppy stems of flowers, light lavender-blue, and grows to 12in tall.

Sow seed in spring or increase by division then. Zones 3–8.

Campsis

HARDY CLIMBERS   Glorious self-clinging vines with rich trumpet flowers and finely cut deciduous foliage. Good on walls, pergolas, arbors and arches, in a warm and sunny situation. The soil or potting mix should be moisture retentive but well drained. Keep in shape by cutting back to a pair of buds as required.

Campsis grandiflora, deep orange-red blooms 29½–33ft. *C.* x *tagliabuana* 'Mme Galen', salmon-red blooms 33–39ft. *C. radicans*, scarlet blooms 39–49ft.

Propagate by heeled cuttings in early fall. Zones 5–9.

Caryopteris

HARDY DECIDUOUS SHRUB   Shrubby plants with blue flowers, caryopteris make lovely raised border plants for edging a patio, or even as specimen plants on their own in a patio paving space. The flower color contrasts well with warm paving, or terracotta containers. A sunny site and well draining soil or potting mix is needed.

Caryopteris x *clandonensis* has several

varieties which differ mainly in the shade of blue. Caryopteris will grow up to about 4ft, but are usually kept compact and bushy by cutting back to 2ft or so.

Increase by heeled cuttings in early fall. Zones 6–8.

Ceanothus

HARDY DECIDUOUS AND EVERGREEN SHRUBS   Most of the Californian lilacs have bluish flowers. They make excellent wall shrubs and a few grow well as sprawling plants for draping over steps, paving or container edges. A sunny site, sheltered and with well drained soil or potting mix is required.

Ceanothus 'Autumnal Blue', blue flowers, summer and autumn, glossy evergreen foliage, 8ft, or more, good against a wall. *C.* 'Delight', rich blue flowers in spring, evergreen, to 8ft. *C.* 'Gloire de Versailles', powder blue flowers in autumn, deciduous, to 6½ft. *C. gloriosus*, deep purple-blue flowers, evergreen carpeter, 4–12in. *C. griseus*, lilac-blue, evergreen, 6–8in. *C. thyrsiflorus* 'Repens', ground cover evergreen covered with flowers, 3ft.

Increase by cuttings in spring and summer, the species also by seed. Zones 8–10.

Centaurea

TENDER HERBACEOUS PERENNIAL   This dusty miller is a brilliantly silver-foliaged plant, making an excellent contrast to brightly colored flowers or against stone.

Left The trumpet vine, *Campsis radicans* produces self-clinging aerial roots which will cover a patio wall or a pergola. Scarlet and orange blooms will appear in August and September

A good plant on its own or in groups. Grow in well drained soil or potting mix, in a sunny position. Lift and pot those growing in the ground and keep them, and pot grown ones, in a frost-free place overwinter, if required for the next year. *Centaurea gymnocarpa* is a shrubby evergreen with silver, ferny foliage, 18–30in.

Increase by fall cuttings. Zones 4–9.

Centranthus

HARDY HERBACEOUS PERENNIAL If you do not mind a perennial plant that will probably spread, filling in any available crevices, the red valerian is a good choice. It grows well in dry positions, even walls, in sun or light shade, often where little else will grow. A long flowering season, attracts butterflies.

Centranthus ruber, though called the red valerian, has heads of crimson, red, pink, or white flowers in summer, rather fleshy gray-green leaves, and grows 18–36in tall.

Increase by basal cuttings in late spring or raise from seed in spring or fall. Zones 4–9.

Below A sub shrub, *Ceratostigma plumbaginoides* grows well in walls, between paving, or as ground cover in a bed. Its valuable qualities are a long flowering period, July to November, and red tinted leaves in fall

Cerastium

HARDY HERBACEOUS PERENNIAL Snow-in-summer is another invasive plant but, unlike centranthus, forms large creeping mats which become smothered with flower through the summer. It will grow in cracks and crevices, in walls, gravel and paving, in windowboxes and hanging baskets, in sun and any soil.

Cerastium tomentosum has masses of white flowers from late spring into summer above grayish to white mats of foliage, 4–6in high.

Increase by division or cuttings in spring. Zones 2–3.

Ceratostigma

HARDY HERBACEOUS PERENNIALS OR SHRUBS Of the two plants described here, both of which flower from summer into fall, one is a deciduous, shrubby plant, the other a spreading, herbaceous perennial. Both need a sunny and sheltered position, and are splendid around the base of a patio wall where their blue

flowers contrast well with warm stone.

Ceratostigma plumbaginoides, blue plumbago, is an herbaceous perennial with leaves which colors well in the fall spreading, 1ft. *C. willmottianum*, Chinese plumbago, shrubby but will behave as an herbaceous perennial in cold areas, some fall color, 2–4ft.

Increase by division in spring, Chinese plumbago can also be propagated by semi-ripe cuttings in late fall. Zones 6–8.

Chaenomeles

HARDY DECIDUOUS SHRUBS The flowering quinces, noted for their spring blossoms, are superb wall shrubs. Good against the house wall or growing over a patio wall from a surrounding bed. Almost any soil or situation will be accepted. Besides the delightful flowers, in shades of crimson, scarlet, pink and white, the fruit of most varieties makes an excellent conserve.

Chaenomeles japonica, low spreading, 3ft tall. *C. speciosa* varieties are spreading shrubs, about 5–10ft tall. *C.* x *superba* varieties also spread but are generally less tall at 3–5ft.

Increase by layering in spring. Zone 5.

Chamaecyparis

HARDY CONIFERS Probably best known as fast-growing hedging plants which quickly make enemies of neighbors, there are, however, several delightful false cypresses that are dwarf, slow growing or columnar in shape. They will do well in sun or partial shade. Being evergreen they are useful all year round as accent plants on patios, in windowboxes, and bordering steps. Use a peat-based mix.

Heights and widths of the following varieties are approximations. *C. lawsoniana* varieties: 'Aurea Densa', makes a small roundish bush of golden yellow, about 2ft after 10 years; 'Chilworth Silver', a silvery blue column 6ft high by 2ft wide after 10 years; 'Gimbornii', very compact, dense rounded blue green bush some 2ft after 10 years; 'Tamariscifolia', green blue, only about 3ft high but over 6½ft wide in flat sprays. Of the *C. obtusa* varieties, 'Caespitosa' is a tiny plant suitable for pots and windowboxes, deep green, up to 4in high and wide; 'Nana', has dense blackish-green flat sprays, to about 10in high but a little

wider in 10 years. *C. pisifera* varieties, 'Boulevard', silver-blue column to 6½ft in 10 years but eventually 16ft or so, so keep trimmed to shape; 'Squarrosa Sulphurea', pale yellow spring to summer, variable growth up to about 6½ by 3ft in 10 years.

Increase by heeled cuttings in early fall. Zones 4–8.

Cheiranthus

GROWN AS BIENNIALS The spring scent of wallflowers in a patio bed, container or windowbox is a real delight. Tall varieties make good cut flowers. Easy to grow, but don't plant in the same bed more than one year in three. They are grown as biennials, but see *Erysimum* also for the perennial kind. They do best in sun.

Cheiranthus cheiri has many strains, mostly well scented, in shades of crimson, brownish reds, orange, yellow, buff and cream, they grow 10–18in tall.

Increase by seed sown in late spring or early summer or buy young plants in the fall. Zones 7–9.

Chionodoxa

HARDY BULBS Lovely early spring flowering bulbs for underplanting taller plants such as small conifers. Glory of the

Above The rock rose, cistus, has single saucer shaped blooms which may appear and be shed in a day. So many buds are set, however, that there is a long succession of flowers during the spring and summer

snow is suitable for growing in patio spaces in soil or in any outdoor containers of potting mix, in sun or light shade.

Chionodoxa luciliae has bright blue flowers with a white eye. The flowers are white in 'Alba', pale gentian blue in 'Gigantea', large pink in 'Pink Giant', the tallest variety, and lilac-rose in 'Rosea', 3–8in tall. *C. sardensis* has good gentian blue flowers, with or without a small white eye, about 5in.

Increase by lifting and dividing the bulb offsets when dormant. Zones 4–9.

Cistus

HARDY OR NEARLY HARDY EVERGREEN SHRUBS Lovely green or gray leaved shrubs with tissue-paper-like flowers. The sun roses demand a warm, sheltered and well drained site, such as may be provided on a patio, in a space in the paving, walled bed or in a container. Most are not completely hardy and may be damaged in severe, wet winters.

Cistus x *corbariensis*, white, yellow-eyed flowers, dark green leaves, 2–3ft tall but wider, is one of the hardiest. *C.* x *cyprius*, white flowers with blood-red spots, dark green to grayish leaves, is 6ft tall but spreads more; fairly hardy. *C. monspeliensis* has white flowers borne in profusion, narrow leaves, 2–4ft tall, spreading. *C. parviflorus*, puce pink, grayish downy leaves, to 3ft tall. *C.*

'Silver Pink', silvery pink, gray green leaves, to 2½ft tall; fairly hardy.

Grow species from seed in spring and hybrids from heeled cuttings in early fall. Zones 8–10.

Clematis

HARDY EVERGREEN AND DECIDUOUS CLIMBERS There are clematis for most positions on the patio, from strong climbers to decorate walls, arbors and arches, to pillar climbers and sprawling plants to drape over the edges of steps and containers. All prefer cool, moist soil from where they may grow or climb into the sun. Wherever they are planted, therefore, do make sure that they have sufficient moisture retentive soil or potting mix, add peat if necessary and cover the soil surface over the plant's roots with tiles, stones or gravel. Prune species as required to keep them in shape and always remove dead wood. Prune the large-flowered hybrids which flower in early summer after flowering, and late summer and fall flowering species in spring. Most clematis are deciduous with only a few evergreen or nearly so.

Clematis alpina, one of the most charming of plants with 6ft trailing stems, is lovely sprawling over stones, paving or steps, and carries lavender-blue flowers in spring; it has blue, white and rose varieties. *C. armandii*, an evergreen needing a sheltered wall site, has white scented flowers in spring, and the variety 'Apple Blossom' has pink-tipped blooms. C. florida 'Sieboldii' (C. f. 'Bicolor') has white flowers with a purple-violet rosette in the centre, summer to the fall, nearly evergreen, short climber for patio or trellis, 6–10ft. C. macropetala has violet or rose semi-double flowers from late spring to summer, for pillar or trellis, 6–11½ft. C. montana, a rampant deciduous climber for walls and large structures, such as pergolas, flowers from late spring into summer, pink in 'Elizabeth', rose in 'Rubens', white and scented in 'Wilsonii', which is also later flowering. C. orientalis is a rampant climber able to smother a pergola or arbor, from which its nodding, thick-petalled yellow flowers may hang from early summer well into fall when they mingle with the silver seed heads of the earlier flowers. It is deciduous, growing to 19½–23ft.

Most of the hybrid clematis have large flowers in a wide range of color; the list is being continually added to and selection is very much a matter of personal preference. The old favourites of 'Jackmanii', deep violet, 'Nelly Moser', lilac pink with rose bar, are excellent and hard to beat but other colors and forms may be more acceptable for your purpose.

Increase by summer cuttings or layering in spring or early summer. Zones 5–9.

Cleome

HALF-HARDY ANNUAL An aromatic plant for a sunny spot. It has interesting flower heads, the long stamens and petal positions giving rise to the name of spider flower. Grow in beds surrounding a patio or a group of plants as a feature in a patio paving space, in good soil. This is one of the best of the not so well known and grown annual plants.

Cleome spinosa has flowers ranging from pale to rich pinks, purple and white, and grows 2–3ft.

Sow seed in spring indoors. Zones 4–9.

Left Clematis is a classic, decorative, trailer plant. Here *C. macropetala* 'Maidwell Hall' spills its deep blue lampshade flowers from its container, an earthenware wine vessel

Above The sharply defined patterns of the petals of *Convolvulus minor* 'Dwarf Rainbow Flash' make a strong statement. They are held on an erect, bushy plant, useful for growing between rocks and stones

Convolvulus

HARDY ANNUALS   For a splash of color a mixed selection of the dwarf convolvulus is hard to beat, since they will quickly fill up a patio space or windowbox. Not fussy about soil or potting mix, they do like sun.

Convolvulus tricolor has flowers of pink, red or blue, with white and yellow eyes, and grows 6–12in according to the strain; individual colors, usually blues, and mixed strains are available.

Sow seed in spring. Zone 5.

Cosmos

HALF-HARDY ANNUALS   Elegant plants with bright flowers and finely divided leaves which are excellent for a gay summer show in patio borders or surrounding beds. Sun and most soils, especially sandy ones, are acceptable.

Cosmos bipinnatus has flowers in shades of pink, rose, carmine and white, or white splashed crimson, according to variety, and single or double blooms, 1½–4ft tall. *C. sulphureus* varieties are in yellow, red, orange or white, single or double blooms, 1–3ft tall.

Raise from seeds sown indoors in spring. Zones 4–9.

Cotoneaster

HARDY DECIDUOUS OR EVERGREEN SHRUBS Several of the cotoneasters are very useful, either as accent plants growing in a patio space, or backing against a wall. Most well drained soils in sun or light shade will be accepted.

Cotoneaster adpressus is a fine prostrate crack filler, slow growing to 18in tall but 3ft or more across, deciduous leaves turn red in the fall. *C. congestus*, dense evergreen, forming a creeping mound, up to about 10in tall and wider, suitable for covering paving and tumbling over steps. *C. horizontalis*, a popular deciduous shrub for walls where the herringbone branch formation is shown off to advantage, leaves often color well in the fall and the plants may berry well — red, to 5ft tall.

Increase by seed in spring or heeled cuttings in early fall. Zones 5–9.

Cymbalaria

HARDY HERBACEOUS PERENNIAL A lovely little perennial for dry walls, cracks or other impossible places that need filling, as well as hanging baskets and windowboxes. It will endure shade but flowers best in sun.

Cymbalaria muralis (Linaria cymbalaria), the ivy-leaved toadflax, has trailing stems up to some 2ft long with lilac and yellow flowers from spring to the fall, and deep green roundish, ivy-shaped leaves. It can be invasive, but is less so in the even smaller variety 'Nana Alba', which has white and yellow flowers.

Sow seed in spring or increase by division then. Zones 3–7.

Cytisus

HARDY DECIDUOUS SHRUBS Brooms of various sorts make ideal patio plants, breaking up the plainness or straightness of walls, tumbling over containers or steps. Most are evergreen stemmed and of interest all the year round. Grow in sun and well drained soil.

Cytisus battandieri, pineapple broom, has pineapple-scented yellow flowers in dense clusters, silvery green deciduous to semi-evergreen leaves, 11–13ft tall, best and loveliest against a wall. *C. x beanii*, gold flowers, is 12–14in tall but sprawling, good over steps, in raised beds or urns. *C. scoparius*, Scotch broom, has varieties with a wide range of flower color and many bicolors; most grow 5–8ft tall and are good against walls.

Increase by spring-sown seed or take heeled cuttings in fall. Brooms resent root disturbance. Zones 6–10.

Dianthus

HARDY HERBACEOUS PERENNIALS Pinks are among the most useful of patio plants. They will grow in paving cracks or in small patio beds where their light blue-green leaves set off against the stone, or do equally well with their backs to a wall but they do best in a sunny position.

Dianthus x *allwoodii*, the modern garden pink, is usually rather short lived. There are many varieties of this, mostly growing between 10–16in tall, and in a very wide array of colors. Dwarf forms making mats about 4in high are 'Albus', white with a purple-spotted centre, and 'Red Velvet', deep crimson, blackish centre. *D. deltoides*, maiden pink, is an ideal crevice plant for use in walls and paving. It flowers through summer, is 6–10in tall, and has varieties 'Albus', white, crimson eye; 'Brilliant', rose pink; 'Samos', carmine, dark leaves.

Increase by cuttings in summer. Zones 3–8.

Dimorphotheca

HARDY ANNUALS The botanists now include *Osteospermum* under this name and there are some very bright and lovely hybrids offered in seed catalogs. Grow them in small patio beds, urns or windowboxes, in a sunny and sheltered position if possible, treating them as annuals. The daisy blooms unfold in sun, and are reluctant to open in shade or on dull days. The hybrids include 'Dwarf Salmon', apricot pink, 9in; 'Giant Mixed', in shades of cream, salmon and orange, 12in; 'Tetra Pole Star', shining white, violet centred, 18in.

Sow seed in spring. Zones 4–9.

Doronicum

HARDY HERBACEOUS PERENNIALS Fine early spring flowering plants with large yellow daisy flowers, the leopard's banes are all rather similar and vary mainly in height. They need moisture

retentive soil or potting mix and do well in sun or light shade. Most varieties make good long-lasting cut flowers.

The lower growing ones described here are good as a border edging, and for filling containers or windowboxes. *D. austriacum*, 1½–2ft; *D. cordatum (D. caucasicum, D. columnae)*, 6–12in; varieties and hybrids include 'Magnificum', large flowers, 18–24in; 'Miss Mason', very floriferous, 18in; 'Spring Beauty', double flowers, 16in.

Increase by division from the fall to spring or by spring sown seed. Zones 4–9.

Dryopteris

HARDY FERNS The buckler ferns include both evergreen and deciduous species. Though sun is acceptable they are good in shady, cool spots, such as may be found in some patio corners or on the sunless sides of walls, or as underplanting in permanent schemes. Humus-rich soil or potting mix is best.

Dryopteris aemula, the hay scented buckler fern, gets its name from the fragrant, bright green fronds, 6–24in long, evergreen. *D. cristata*, crested buckler fern, has fertile fronds with the leaflets twisted into a horizontal position, 2–3ft long, the sterile fronds 1–1½ft, deciduous, good in moist spots. *D. filix-*

Above Reluctant to open in a dull spot or in shade the daisy flowers of the Cape marigold, dimorphotheca, are best cultivated in a sunny position. The plant does well in pots and windowboxes

Above Eccremocarpus is a useful evergreen vine which will climb a vertical surface and then branch out, a quality that makes it ideal for covering pergolas

mas, the male fern, has rich green deciduous to semi-evergreen fronds, 1–4ft long; it has a number of varieties with crisped and crested fronds; good in poor and dry conditions.

Increase by division in the fall or spring. Zones 3–4.

Eccremocarpus

HALF HARDY CLIMBER The Chilean glory flower is an evergreen perennial vine which may die back in harsh winter conditions or even die out altogether. However, it is easily raised annually from seed and so can be grown as an annual in cold areas. Its long flowering season and self-clinging habit make it a very useful vine for walls, trellises and arbors or for trailing over a low wall. Most soils are accepted.

Eccremocarpus scaber, brilliant orange to red flowers from late spring into the fall, climbs 10–19½ft. Once raised from spring-sown seed it will usually seed itself in future years. Zones 8–10.

Erica

HARDY EVERGREEN SHRUBS The heaths will do well in containers and, for the acid-loving varieties, suitably prepared pockets of non-alkaline soil or potting mix should be provided. Use prepared rhododendron mix or peat as required. Trim over with shears after flowering to keep them compact. The heaths are floriferous, low growing, evergreen shrubs with flowers in shades of purple, carmine, pink, rose and white. Some of them have attractively colored foliage varying from green to yellow.

There are many species and hybrids including the few mentioned here. *E. cinerea*, bell heather, dislikes lime, flowers in summer to the fall, and most varieties grow 8–12in; 'Alba Minor', white flowers, light green foliage, 6in; 'Atrosanguinea Smiths Variety', profuse bright rose-pink flowers set off against dark green foliage; 'Foxhollow Mahogany', mahogany rose, dark green foliage; 'Golden Drop', not noted for its few pink flowers but for its coppery gold leaves which turn brownish red in winter; 'Golden Hue', pink flowers, coppery gold leaves flushed reddish in winter, to 20in; 'Velvet Night', very dark, blackish-purple flowers over deep green leaves.

Erica herbacea (E. carnea), winter heath, lime tolerant, flowers winter to spring, most varieties grow 10–12in tall, 'Aurea', pink to almost white flowers, golden foliage; 'Myretoun Ruby' ('Winter Jewel'), ruby-red flowers over dark foliage; 'Ruby Glow', dark red flowers, bronze-green foliage; 'Snow Queen', white, bright green leaves; 'Springwood Pink', rose; 'Springwood White', white, bright green leaves, rampant and may become invasive; 'Vivellii', carmine, bronzy winter foliage.

Increase by heeled cuttings in summer. Zones 5–8.

Erigeron

HARDY HERBACEOUS PERENNIALS Fleabanes resemble Michaelmas daisies (*Aster*), but have more flower petals, some are yellow flowered. Most varieties are shades of purple, mauve, violet-blue, lilac and pink. All make excellent long-lasting cut flowers, and many are dwarf plants. For sunny sites, the dwarf forms make excellent crevice fillers in paving and need gritty soils or potting mixes; the taller sorts are useful in containers or patio beds.

Good kinds include *E. aurantiacus*, orange or yellow flowers, clump forming, 8–10in; *E. aureus*, deep yellow flowers, clump forming, 3–4in; *E. borealis (E. alpinus)*, purple, yellow-centred flowers, tufted, 4–8in; and many brilliant hybrids, which grow to a height of 2–2½ft. *E. karvinskianus (E. mucronatus)*, 4–6in, has white to pale pink flowers, spreads wildly and is good in walls and paving cracks. All are summer flowering.

Increase from the fall to spring by division or sow seed in spring. Zones 3–8.

Erysimum

HARDY HERBACEOUS PERENNIALS Some of these are grown as biennials. They are very similar to wallflowers (*Cheiranthus* spp) and need the same conditions. *E.* x *allionii (Cheiranthus* x *allionii)*, Siberian wallflower, orange to yellow, 12–16in, perennial grown as a biennial. *E. alpinum*, scented sulphur-yellow flowers, or primrose yellow in 'Moonlight', 6in, perennial. *E. linifolium*, lilac to violet flowers, 8–18in, perennial grown as a biennial.

Sow seed from late spring to early summer. Zones 7–9.

Escallonia

HARDY EVERGREEN SHRUBS Fine shrubs with which to hedge a patio or they may be grown against a wall. Accept shearing and will still produce flowers. Grow in most reasonable soils and sun. Excellent in mild coastal areas, but avoid very cold sites.

The hybrids of *E.* x *langleyensis (E.* x *rigida)* include the most popular escallonias, most grow about 6½ft tall, and include 'Apple Blossom', pink and white, 5ft; 'Donard Seedling', pink buds and white flowers; 'Donard Star', deep rose; 'Peach Blossom', deep pink; 'Slieve Donard', pale pink with carmine markings.

Increase by heeled cuttings in late summer or early fall. Zones 8–10.

Euonymus

EVERGEEEN AND DECIDUOUS SHRUBS AND TREES Some of the spindles are admirably adapted as patio specimens. Many of the evergreen species and varieties have variegated leaves and many are good scrambling or trailing plants, useful for cascading over low walls, steps or from windowboxes. Grow in any good soil, or potting mix, in sun or light shade. Trim only as required to keep them in bounds.

Euonymus alatus, deciduous, the leaves turn to brilliant autumn colors, may grow where maples fail, 3–6½ft tall and as broad or more. *E. europaeus*, spindle tree, a fine small deciduous tree, 10ft or more tall and as wide, good fall foliage color, bright pink and orange fruit; it has several varieties varying in fruit and leaf color. *E. fortunei*, an evergreen species which trails without support, the stems are some 6ft long; has several varieties varying in leaf shape and with variegations of silver or yellow.

Increase by heeled cuttings late spring, late summer, or early fall; species also by seed. Zones 4–7.

Euphorbia

HARDY HERBACEOUS PERENNIALS, EVERGREEN SHRUBS Some of the many spurges make good patio plants. Most grow best in a sunny spot and in most soils or potting mix, and need space to spread.

Euphorbia characias is a shrubby evergreen, 2–5ft tall, with gray-green leaves and yellowish-green and maroon-brown flower heads. *E. epithymoides (E. polychroma)*, an herbaceous perennial, 1–2ft tall, has bright green leaves turning reddish and yellow-green flower heads, and forms clumps. *E. griffithii*, herbaceous perennial, 2½–3ft, with rather willow-like grayish green leaves and bright reddish flower heads, forming clumps.

Increase by division of clumps or by seed sown in spring. Zones 5–8.

Fatsia

EVERGREEN SHRUB A splendid specimen shrub for a sheltered patio, in a sunny or shady spot. Grow in good soil, or potting mix if tub grown.

Fatsia japonica 'Variegata' is the most

Left Carrying evergreen, palmate leaves which have a glossy sheen and white flower umbels in fall, fatsia is a welcome addition to a patio, grown either as a border shrub or as a movable pot plant

interesting form with large fig-like leaves, deep green margined white. Whitish bobbles of flowers in the fall give it an unusual, almost exotic look. Grows up to 6ft and as wide. Increase by cuttings in early fall. Zones 7–8.

Festuca

HARDY GRASS Ornamental grass which offers permanent patio interest in either a paving space or as an edging. Choose a sunny or only lightly shaded spot and good soil.

Festuca glauca (F. ovina glauca), the blue fescue, makes dense tufts of blue-gray leaves which contrast well with warm colored paving or pebbles. It grows about 6–10in and as broad.

Increase by division in spring or the fall. Zones 4–8.

Fuchsia

HARDY OR HALF-HARDY SHRUBS Spectacular blooming shrubs, mainly evergreen when grown frost free but otherwise deciduous in the open. There are fuchsias for every patio situation, windowbox or hanging basket. Use good soil if planted in the ground and grow in sun or partial shade. Many varieties may be trained as standards but they, and other tender varieties outdoors, will need to be grown on in a frost-free place over-winter to survive. In cool areas it is wise to protect the base of the hardier, planted out fuchsias with peat or bark chippings to about 6in deep. In mild areas the hardier fuchsias may be used as hedging.

There are about a hundred species and hundreds more hybrids; most grow 3–6ft tall, but there are some very good, lower growing ones too. *F. magellanica*, the hardiest fuchsia, is deciduous, up to 10ft or more in mild areas, excellent for hedging or planting in patio beds, and has red and purple flowers; it has several good varieties of which 'Pumila', red and violet, 8in, is very good in window boxes and hanging baskets; so, too, is 'Alice Hoffman', rose red and white, compact, about 6–10in, with bronze-tinged leaves. 'Cascade' is a tender, weeping variety, flowers pink flushed white and red, which is superb for hanging baskets, tumbling over urns, windowboxes or other containers which can be brought in over winter. Prune established plants in spring.

All are easy to increase by cuttings in summer; when rooted and growing, pinch out the growing tips, and repeat as necessary to produce bushy plants. There are good hybrid seeds available too. Zones 5–9.

Galanthus

HARDY BULB The snowdrops are delightful little bulbous plants, perfectly hardy and excellent as early-flowering windowbox inhabitants or in a patio patch. They do best in fairly rich soil or potting mix and will thrive in lightly shaded spots.

There are many species and varieties, varying in flower and leaf size or height, but few have the grace of the common snowdrop *G. nivalis*. This flowers from January onwards, depending on weather and warmth, grows 4–8in, and has a double form, 'Plena'.

Below A deep red fuchsia contained in a hanging basket complements the honey tones of this wooden pergola

Increase by offset bulbs, which are freely produced, after flowering. Zone 3.

Geranium

HARDY HERBACEOUS PERENNIALS The true geranium species, cranesbills, are perennial plants with blooms in shades of blue, mauve, purple, lilac, rose, pink and near white. They are of variable size and habit but most form good, spreading clumps. They are excellent bed fillers, good for surrounding plants such as columnar conifers in a permanent setting of a raised or surrounding bed. Some are also good for containers or small patio paving spaces. Grow in any reasonable soil or potting mix and in sun or only light shade. Useful, easily grown and long flowering plants.

There are many species and varieties including *G. endressii*, pink flowers from summer into the fall, forms great spreading mats of limitless width if allowed, to 15in high, a quick space filler or coverer. *G. himalayense (G. grandiflorum)*, violet-blue flowers, early summer, leaves may color in the fall, forms mats to 12in tall, and *G. wallichianum*, violet-blue flowers, summer to the fall, forming tufts, about 6–10in or so high; flowers bluish with a large white eye in the variety 'Buxton's Blue'.

Increase by division in the fall or spring. Zones 4–7.

Glechoma (Nepeta)

HARDY HERBACEOUS PERENNIAL The variegated form of ground ivy is an excellent evergreen perennial for hanging baskets or windowboxes and also forms useful mats for ground cover. It has long trailing stems which will scramble over stones and over the edges of any container, and will grow in sun or shade and in any ordinary soil or potting mix. Best in mild areas.

Glechoma hederacea 'Variegata', prostrate and rooting along the stem at leaf joints, has leaves splashed and streaked white, and insignificant purplish blooms.

Increase by division in spring or cuttings from spring to the fall. Zones 4–7.

Hebe

HARDY OR SLIGHTLY TENDER EVERGREEN SHRUBS There are many differ-

ent types of hebe which are suitable for a range of patio situations, windowboxes or other containers. They are fine evergreen shrubs, varying in hardiness, some indeed rather tender and needing a sheltered site, others surviving more easily in towns and yet others that are quite hardy. Grow in sun, in well drained soil or potting mix, the large shrubs in a warm and sheltered spot, while the dwarf forms described here are generally hardier and will grow in open areas, such as patio beds. Attractive flowers make a spring bonus.

Species include *H. albicans*, white flowers, gray-green rounded leaves to 2ft or more tall, twice as much across. *H. armstrongii*, a foliage plant, the leaves yellowish green, small and close pressed to the stems and giving a rather scaly, whipcord appearance, to about 3ft, an interesting plant for a sheltered position. *H. pinguifolia*, white flowers and blue-gray leaves on a bushy plant to about 1½ft; the variety 'Pagei' is similar but more compact to about 6–10in and mat forming. There are also many hybrids which vary in flower color and height.

Increase by summer cuttings. Zone 9.

Hedera

MOSTLY HARDY EVERGREEN CLIMBERS The English ivies are some of the hardiest of plants, accepting most situations, good in hanging baskets, windowboxes, in fact most containers, as well as providing wall cover. Mainly evergreen, climbing or ground covering

Above Free blooming and spreading in clumps *Geranium atlanticum* is excellent as a summer ground cover, for growing along steps and beside walls

Above The exotic, trumpet shaped and yellow throated blooms of *Hemerocallis* 'Pink Damask', the day lily, will look good if treated as accent flowers on the patio

Numerous hybrids are now available with flowers from cream, clear to deep yellow, apricot and peachy colors, oranges, pinks, light to deep reds and brownish colours, some are bicolored too — usually three petals of one color, three of another. They vary in height from about 16–48in. Choice must depend on the site available and your own color preference. Two very popular and reliable hybrids are 'Pink Damask', a warm rose pink and 'Stafford', a deep red with a yellow eye, and both grow to about 30–36in tall. Many yellow-flowered hybrids are very well scented but not many of the modern ones have the scent of 'Dorothy McDade', with waxy, clear yellow flowers and about 2½ft tall.

Divide the clumps in spring or the fall. Zones 3–9.

Hepatica

ROCK PLANT A lovely early-flowering plant, suitable for shady areas either underplanting deciduous shrubs in a bed or in pans and troughs, including window-boxes. Use good, rich soil or potting mix, and ideally well lined if possible. *H. nobilis (H. triloba)*, has masses of Wedgwood-blue flowers in early spring over three-lobed, almost evergreen leaves, 3–4in tall.

Increase by division in spring or the fall or seed sown when ripe; established plants will seed themselves. Zone 4.

Hosta

HARDY HERBACEOUS PERENNIALS Very bold leafed foliage plants, the plantain lilies are excellent in a lightly shaded or sunny patio paving space, as a feature, or as edging where they can be left to develop into large clumps. They prefer a moist and well drained soil or potting mix.

There are many species and varieties, often rather similar. *H. fortunei* 'Albo-picta' has strong leaves, yellow edged with pale green in early spring but the variegation gradually changes until the leaves are all green, lilac flowers in 12in spikes to 2ft tall. *H. plantaginea* 'Grandi-flora', gray-green leaves, well scented white flowers in spikes to about 2ft. *H. sieboldiana (H. glauca)*, large gray-blue leaves, to 2ft 'Elegans' bears pale lilac flowers in short spikes.

Increase by division of the plants in

plants, they need reasonable soil or potting mix and a sunny or shady position.

Hedera canariensis 'Gloire de Marengo' is not fully hardy so should be regarded as a short-stay plant for a hanging basket or windowbox, and may also be grown against a sheltered wall. It has large gray-green and green leaves splashed with cream. *H. colchica* 'Variegata' is hardy, vigorous, otherwise rather similar to 'Gloire de Marengo' but with larger leaves. *H. helix*, the English ivy, has many good forms including 'Buttercup', yellow leaves edged with green; 'Glacier', green, gray and white leaves; 'Goldheart', dark green, yellow-centred leaves, pink young stems 'Tricolor' ('Marginata Elegantissima'), small leaves variegated cream, pink tinged — particularly in cold weather.

Increase by cuttings in summer. Zones 5–9.

Hemerocallis

HARDY HERBACEOUS PERENNIALS The deciduous day lilies will grow anywhere — sun or shade, dryish or moist soil. Admirable for any patio bed, they are very good as accent plants in a patio paving space too. Their leaves emerge lemon green in early spring and, turning green, arch over, lasting through to winter. They form strong clumps.

spring or the fall. Zones 3–9.

Hyacinthus

HARDY BULBS Favorite Christmas-flowering indoor bulbs, the hyacinths also make good flowering bulbs for outdoors — though they will not flower outside at that time. Welcome as early color they make lovely plants to grow grouped in windowboxes and patio beds and spaces. For sun and good soil or potting mix; bulbs which have been forced for Christmas flowering will take at least one year or so to flower properly again when planted out. Bulbs left undisturbed will gradually form clumps. Plant them where their scent can waft indoors, or be enjoyed on the patio.

There are many named varieties available in shades of blue, pink, apricot, yellow and white, 8–12in tall.

Increase by offsets. Zones 6–9.

Hydrangea

HARDY DECIDUOUS SHRUBS AND CLIMBERS The showy hydrangeas are fine, large, flowering shrubs for containers and they may also be used to make a bright windowbox or patio feature. Besides the usual pink, blue and white varieties there are one or two species with other interesting advantages, such

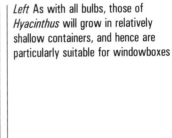

Left As with all bulbs, those of *Hyacinthus* will grow in relatively shallow containers, and hence are particularly suitable for windowboxes

as scent, attractive foliage or climbing ability, and these are admirable for a permanent patio display. Use good moisture retentive soil or potting mix. Grow in a sunny to partially shaded site, which is sheltered if you want the finest blooms. Prune annually to keep tidy and remove spent flower heads in spring; thinning out every 2 to 3 years by removing old shoots nearly to the base may encourage vigorous new growth of all except *H. petiolaris.*

Hydrangea petiolaris (H. scandens), the Japanese climbing hydrangea, a fine self-clinging plant which eventually reaches a height of about 49–66ft,

Left For low level dramatic effect few foliage plants can beat the generously leaved herbaceous hostas. Here *Hosta sieboldiana* provides a blue companion to a striped *H. undulata*

Above An embellished but not over fussy terracotta pot complements the great, flat, flower corymbs of *Hydrangea macrophylla*, a native of China and Japan

creamy white flowers carried in flat heads like a lace cap hydrangea, the leaves turn bright yellow in the fall; may be used to scramble over low surrounding walls instead of climbing up a support. *H. macrophylla (H. hortensis)*, the house hydrangea, has many excellent varieties in shades of pink to carmine some of which turn blue to violet in suitable soil (or may be so turned with a blueing chemical) and white flushed with pink or green. Large round heads of blooms, although in the lace cap type these are flatter and have small central flowers surrounded by the larger sterile ones. Most grow to about 6½ft if left undisturbed in the ground. *H. paniculata* is a splendid shrub as accent plant with huge cone-shaped sprays of flower in cream tinged with pink, honey scented, on arching branches, reaching 8–11ft eventually.

Increase by cuttings in spring and early summer. Zones 6–9.

Hypericum

HARDY EVERGREEN SHRUBS AND ROCK PLANTS Although there are many herbaceous St John's worts, the shrubby species and varieties provide some very useful patio and container plants. Most require a sunny to partially shaded site and any reasonable soil or potting mix. The larger shrubs are good for a patio surround, dense and floriferous, while the creeping ones may grow well where other plants might not, in and over gravel beds, as wall plants and even drape from hanging baskets or windowboxes. All have yellow flowers in summer, many with a central tuft of deep gold stamens. Berried varieties are much sought after by flower arrangers in the fall. Most are evergreen or nearly so, depending on the severity of the winter.

In *H. androsaemum*, tutsan, the heads of flowers are followed by bright red berries which turn black. Deciduous, 24–30in, tolerates shade and will grow from paving cracks. *H. calycinum*, rose of Sharon, a common but first rate creeping plant covered with large yellow flowers in summer and fall, needs to be kept in bounds but makes good ground cover, 10–16in, will grow in some shade. *H. cerastoides*, a splendid tufted perennial forming mats of evergreen leaves covered with flowers, is good on walls or paving in sun, to 6in. *H. olympicum*, sometimes offered as *H. polyphyllum*, is also excellent for walls and paving making a spreading mound covered with flowers, to 6in, for sun.

Increase by division and cuttings in summer. Zones 6–9.

Iberis

HARDY ANNUALS AND HERBACEOUS PERENNIALS The candytufts are easy plants that do well in fairly poor soil, which makes them rather good for difficult patio spots. They do well in pockets and crevices between paving stones but do need sun. Recommended are *I. amara*, white flowers in spikes, 16in; scented in the variety 'Giant Hyacinth Flowered', 12–16in. *I. gibraltarica*, perennial, pink flowers in spring, 12in. *I. sempervirens*, perennial, white flowers in spring and summer, semi-evergreen, 8–12in; larger white flowers in 'Snowflake'. *I. umbellata*, annual, flowers in shades of mauve, lilac, carmine, rose, pink and white, 6–12in.

Increase by seed in spring and the perennials by cuttings in early summer. Zones 4–10.

Impatiens

HALF-HARDY PERENNIALS Known also as busy lizzies or patience plants, these are among the easiest of plants to grow,

although they are not winter hardy. Excellent in containers of all sorts and for massing in windowboxes, they require moist soil or potting mix and do well in light shade.

Impatiens wallerana (I. holstii, I. sultanii) has very succulent stems, flowers through summer and fall in a wide range of color — cerise violet, red, scarlet, orange, rose, pink, white and in bicolors — and comes in various sizes according to strain, 6–14in.

Sow seed in early spring; cuttings may also be taken during the growing season and rooted in water. Zones 4–9.

Ipomoea

GROWN AS HALF-HARDY ANNUALS Among the most beautiful summer climbers, the morning glories make a lovely show when twined into trellis or around poles. They may also be used to scramble over low-growing shrubs or drape from hanging baskets. Grow them either in a large container of good potting mix with suitable supports provided, or plant them into moisture-retentive soil in a patio bed. They do best in sun.

There are several good varieties and hybrids which grow about 8–10ft including: 'Early Call Mixed', early, with flowers in shades of red, pink, blue, lilac and violet; 'Flying Saucers', flowers streaked and striped in blue and white; 'Roman Candy' ('Minibar Rose'), a fine plant with many deep cerise-rose flowers edged and eyed white, leaves marbled white, climbs to about 5ft or can be used in hanging baskets and window boxes if the plant tips are pinched out to make bushy mounds, 8–10in tall, from which the stems trail.

Grow from spring-sown seed; the seed coat may need nicking with a penknife to help germination. Zones 4–10.

Jasminum

HARDY AND TENDER SHRUBS AND CLIMBERS The jasmines include many lovely, deciduous and evergreen, plants. You are indeed fortunate if you have a patio where they may be allowed to clamber, sprawl or scramble, perhaps over a low wall or down steps. As climbers they will need support and regular tying in. Plant in a sunny spot and any good soil.

Not all the jasmines are hardy but the following are among the hardiest. *J. beesianum*, rose-pink fragrant flowers, spring to summer, deciduous, climbing 10–11½ft, *J. nudiflorum*, winter jasmine, yellow flowers, winter into spring, deciduous, scrambling, 10–16½ft, tolerant of north-facing walls. *J. officinale*, common jasmine, white, fragrant flowers, summer to the fall, deciduous, twining climber, possibly to 29½ft. *J. parkeri*, yellow summer flowers, hummock forming evergreen, to 12in, suitable for a patio paving space.

Increase by late summer to early fall cuttings. Shorten and thin out growth in spring if necessary. Zones 5–10.

Juniperus (Juniper)

HARDY CONIFERS Some junipers are ideally suited to patios. These are the ones which either grow pencil-thin upwards or spread flatly. Each has attractively colored evergreen foliage, with varieties in anything from steel-blue to bright gold and from rich dark green to golden green. All are aromatic. The berry-like cones provide an added bonus. They need well drained soil and sun.

The many suitable species and varieties include the following, *J. chinensis*, Chinese juniper, has some good forms, in particular 'Obelisk', blue green foliage, 10ft tall by about 4ft wide. *J. communis*, common juniper, also good forms including 'Compressa', dark green foliage, 18 by 6in; 'Depressa Aurea', young leaves gold green, 12 by 40in. *J. horizontalis*, creeping juniper, has many varieties, all spreading, variously colored foliage. *J. virginiana* eastern red cedar 'Skyrocket', blue gray, 20ft × 1ft.

Increase by heeled cuttings in early fall. Zones 2–10.

Left A long term favorite because they are easy to grow, impatiens sit well in tubs on the patio, or in windowboxes. The patience plants (*I. wallerana*) flower from April to October

Below Perhaps rather dull if planted in groups, nonetheless *Juniperus communis* 'Compressa' can be striking as a single feature, contrasting with herbaceous plants on the patio

Kochia

HALF-HARDY ANNUALS The burning bushes described here are annuals, not to be confused with the perennial bush *Dictamnus*. Kochias are excellent, making low temporary hedging or screening plants and also good as single specimens in patio spaces, windowboxes or surrounding beds. Easy to grow, they prefer good soil or potting mix and sun.

Kochia scoparia trichophylla has two main forms, the usual bushy plant to about 2–3ft and the more compact 'Childsii'. Both have green leaves which turn deep fiery purplish-red in the fall. Raise from seed sown in spring indoors. Zones 4–9.

Lavandula

HARDY EVERGREEN SHRUBS One of the best patio-edging plants or for growing in a sunny place in a patio paving bed. With evergreen aromatic foliage and fragrant flowers, these fine dwarf shrubs require good drainage and a sunny position.

Lavandula angustifolia, English lavender, 2–3ft has several forms, 'Alba', warm white flowers; 'Hidcote', violet, compact, 2½ft; 'Munstead', purple blue, compact, 2½ft. *L. stoechas*, French

Below The burning bush, *Kochia scoparia trichophylla* pictured here, is an interesting annual, having bright green bushes of foliage in summer which turn deep red in the fall

lavender, has deep violet flowers topped by a tuft of purple leaf-like bracts, 1½–3ft.

Trim after flowering and increase by cuttings in summer to early fall. Zone 5.

Lewisia

ROCK PLANTS Among the best of wall plants, the evergreen perennial lewisias fill cracks and crannies with their rosettes of leaves and bright heads of flowers in spring. Also useful for paving cracks on a slope but in wetter seasons they may rot away. They need rich but rapid draining soil, dryish after flowering. Increase drainage around the necks during winter by packing round with gravel.

Lewisia cotyledon, a widely variable species with some named forms, has flowers in white, rose to salmon shades, sometimes striped with deeper tones, 6–10in tall and as wide. *L. tweedyi*, similar but the flowers are in warmer pink about 6in high. There are also a number of hybrids with yellow and orange and salmon to brick-red flowers. 'Rosea', vivid pink, is very good.

Increase by division in spring. Zones 5–6.

Lilium

HARDY AND HALF-HARDY BULBS A number of lilies make imposing plants for urns and other large containers. They may also add an air of distinction to a mixed planting, say in a tub. Give them sun or dappled shade and well draining potting mix, add a quarter by bulk of sharp sand to a peat-based mix. Plant generally 6in deep. Some lilies are tricky but those described below should give a good show without much trouble, and only a few of the large numbers of species and hybrids are mentioned.

The modern hybrid ranges provide many first class plants in a wide choice of form and color and are readily available in garden centers and stores. Asiatic hybrids, usually with scented, reflexed flowers, 2–4ft tall, include 'Brandywine', apricot, scented, 'Destiny', lemon, 'Enchantment', fiery red, 'Paprika', crimson, 'Tabasco', brownish red. *L. longiflorum*, Easter lily, large trumpets, strongly scented, needs starting or over-wintering indoors and is easily raised from seed, to 3ft. The Oriental hybrids

with large, mostly spotted flowers, are excellent tub subjects, including 'Crimson Beauty', white spotted and banded rich red, 4ft; 'Imperial Gold', white spotted maroon and banded yellow, 6ft. Trumpet and Aurelian hybrids, 5–6ft tall, including 'Green Magic', white, green-tinted throat, 'Pink Perfection', pink shades.

Increase by dividing large clumps, a necessity with many varieties, every three or four years to keep them healthy; offsets; or rooting bulb scales; *L. longiflorum* also by seed. Zones 3–8.

Lobelia

GROWN AS HALF-HARDY ANNUALS The annually grown lobelias, with their flowers mostly in shades of blue, are indispensable plants for windowboxes, hanging baskets and many container arrangements. Easy to raise and grow, they do best in reasonable soil or potting mix and in sun.

Lobelia erinus has been developed to provide a range of varieties of different habit and flower color, the pendulous types being an excellent choice. Bushy, mound-forming types include 'Cambridge Blue', light blue, 4–5in; 'Crystal Palace', dark blue, 4–5in; 'Mrs Clibran', violet-blue, white eye, 4–5in; 'Rosamund', carmine with a white eye, 5–6in; 'Strings of Pearls', mixed reds, blues and white, 4in; 'White Lady', white, 6in. The above varieties make good edging.

Trailing types are 'Blue Cascade', light blue; 'Cascade Mixed', reds, blues and white; 'Ruby Cascade', carmine; 'Sapphire', dark blue, white eye.

Raise from seed sown in spring indoors. Zones 4–9.

Lonicera

DECIDUOUS OR EVERGREEN CLIMBERS The honeysuckles are among the most delightful of climbing, twining plants for arbors, pergolas, trellises or scrambling over walls. Some are evergreen, some scented, but generally all are easy to grow. Plant in sun or partial shade in good soil or potting mix with the roots preferably in shade. Plant other leafy, low-growing shrubs close-by.

Not all species and varieties are hardy but the following should prove reliable. *L. henryi*, yellow, flushed red flowers, evergreen, 30–33ft. *L. japonica*, Japanese honeysuckle, cream turning yellow, sometimes purple flushed, scented, evergreen or nearly so, 30–33ft, has some varieties, 'Aureoreticulata', gold-netted leaves and not so vigorous; 'Halliana', white turning yellow, strongly scented. *L. periclymenum*, common honeysuckle or woodbine, creamy white often flushed purple, scented, deciduous, to 20ft, has some varieties, 'Belgica', spring flowering, less vigorous; 'Serotina', later and more vigorous.

Increase by cuttings in early fall. Zones 4–9.

Left Lewisias are sun-loving rock plants needing rich, though gravelly soil. They grow well in walls and between paving stones which are readily drained

Below Popular as garden and cut flowers lilies provide striking splashes of color, either mass planted or grown as individuals in pots. 'Enchantment' is a June flowering, vigorous form

Above Mesembryanthemum is a ground hugging plant which thrives on sandy soil in an open, sunny position. A south facing bank fringing a patio would be an ideal home for this annual

Mesembryanthemum

HALF-HARDY ANNUALS Brilliant flowers for a sunny position, the Livingstone daisies will grow in cracks and well drained pots of soil. *M. criniflorum* (*Dorotheanthus bellidiformis*); has crimson, rose, cerise, salmon, apricot and yellow dark-eyed flowers, and grayish, fleshy leaves, 6in.

Raise by seed sown in spring indoors. Zones 4–9.

Muscari

HARDY BULBS Lovely little blue-flowered bulbs for window boxes, permanent edging or filling in around other patio plantings where they provide easy and reliable spring color. Grow in sun or only partial shade, in almost any soil or potting mix. They will soon colonise if left undisturbed.

Muscari armeniacum has deep bright blue flowers with a white rim in spring, but the leaves appear in the fall, to 6–8in; there are several good varieties including 'Blue Spike', a fragrant, double-flowered grape hyacinth, and 'Cantab', pale sky blue. *M. botryoides*, deep sky blue, up to 5–8in, with fragrant flowers, white in the variety 'Album'. *M. tubergenianum*, the Oxford and Cambridge grape hyacinth, flowers pale blue at the top, deeper blue below, to 6in.

Increase by offset bulbs in late summer. Zones 4–9.

Narcissus

HARDY BULBS The daffodils make good temporary container plants for a spot in sun or partial shade. Grow them in a fairly deep container with good drainage holes, planting them in potting mix so that the bulbs are covered with a bulb's depth of soil and there is sufficient soil below to allow the roots to develop. Except in well sheltered positions it is best not to use tall growing varieties or they will get blown down. Fortunately many of the smaller daffodils possess great charm and are often well scented. Feed the bulbs occasionally when in leaf, and give two or three liquid feeds after flowering.

Narcissus asturiensis (N. minimus) is a small yellow trumpet daffodil for a sunny site, very early flowering, about 3–4in. *N. bulbocodium*, the hoop petticoat daffodil, very small fine petals and conspicuous trumpet, very early flowering, up to 4–6in; this has several named varieties varying mainly in the depth of yellow. *N. canaliculatus* is the usually listed name of *N. tazetta italicus*, white reflexed petals and white or yellow cup, several flowers per stem, strongly scented, best in a warm site, about 4–8in. *N. cyclamineus*, strongly reflexed yellow petals and a yellow trumpet make this a quite distinct little daffodil for a partially shaded spot, up to 5–8in. *N. jonquilla*, the jonquil, has several delightful narcissus flowers to each stem, yellow and strongly scented, to 12in. *N. minor*, twisted yellow petals and a yellow trumpet, early flowering, about 4–8in. *N. obvallaris (N. lobularis)*, the Tenby daffodil, bright yellow trumpet daffodil, early, to 12in. *N. poeticus*, poets narcissus, white petals, small red-rimmed yellow cup, strongly scented, late spring flowering, about 12–16in.

Increase by offsets. Zones 4–8.

Nicotiana

HALF-HARDY ANNUALS The flowering tobacco plants have long been favorites for summer color, but try them in a tub or patio paving space where their fragrance can be appreciated from a sitting area. Grow in good soil in a patio bed or potting mix in a container and in a sunny sheltered site.

There are many hybrids which vary in scent considerably, so do check if your main wish is for fragrance. 'Crimson

Rock', bright crimson, up to 24in; 'Domino', available as a mixture or some separate colors, magenta-purple, rose, pink, lime, white and some bicolors, upward facing, scented flowers, reaching 10–12in; 'Lime Green', greenish yellow, to 2½ft; 'Nicki', available mixed or in some separate colors, maroon, red, rose, pink, lime, white, long lasting, scented, compact 10–12in; 'Sensation', mixed, purple, crimson, pink, lemon, white, scented, tall 2–3ft; 'White Bedder' ('Dwarf White Bedder'), large white flowers, scented, good habit 16in. *N. sylvestris* makes a good pot plant with fragrant white blooms, 3–4ft.

Raise annually from seed sown in spring indoors. Zones 4–9.

Passiflora

SLIGHTLY TENDER CLIMBER A deciduous vine, the blue passion flower is hardy enough to grow outside in many areas if not too wet and cold in winter. Grow it over pergolas and trellis work, scrambling over low walls or against the house wall. It will even grow well in containers provided sufficient support is given. Plant in good soil or soil-based potting mix and a sunny position.

Passiflora caerulea has large white, blue and purple flowers, which in good seasons are followed by orange-yellow fruit, the size of chicken eggs, which are edible but not well flavored. The plant grows to about 16½ft. Increase by summer cuttings. Zones 8–10.

Above These trailing, ivy-leaves geraniums are ideal for brightening a plain brick wall

Pelargonium

HALF-HARDY PERENNIALS These are very popular plants for summer display and excellent in containers of all sorts including hanging baskets and windowboxes. For best effect use the upright growers near the centre of the display and trailers near the edges. They are easy to grow and many of the modern varieties are easy to raise from seed, too. The two main types of geranium dealt with here are the zonals and ivy-leaved trailers; the show or regal pelargoniums are generally more difficult subjects, better suited to indoor and specialist growing. Good soil or potting mix and a sunny spot are preferred but geraniums are pretty tolerant of other conditions.

Pelargonium x *hortorum*, the common zonal or bedding geranium, is available in a wide array of flower and leaf color, and size. The smaller varieties are particularly useful for hanging baskets and windowboxes. The range is vast and only a small selection can be given here. Those raised from seed are indicated as 'from seed', but once such plants are raised they may be propagated by cuttings; those available as plants are so described. 'Breakaway', from seed, red or salmon flowers, spreading plants form a mound with up to 20 stems, good in hanging baskets or small containers, to

Left Mixed colors in a show of tobacco plants. The variety *Nicotiana affinis* 'Sensation' produces sweetly scented and compact plant accepting pot culture

8–10in; 'Caroline Schmidt', plants, double rich red flowers, leaves strongly marbled cream, gray and green, vigorous, 12in, 'Hollywood Star', from seed, white-centred, rose-banded flowers, 12in; 'Mrs Henry Cox', plants, salmon-pink flowers, leaves strongly zoned and marked, red, brown, green and yellow, eye-catching 10in; 'Red Black Vesuvius', plants, red flowers, black green leaves, miniature 6in; 'Video', from seed, gives compact, multi-headed plants without pinching, red, salmon, rose, pink and blush, zoned leaves, reliable 8–10in.

Pelargonium peltatum, the ivy-leaved geraniums include the following, all with stems to about 3ft long. 'Beauty of Eastbourne', deep rose flowers; 'Cornell', lilac flowers; 'Crocodile', pink flowers, leaves white netted; 'L'Elegante', lilac-veined white flowers, cream and pink marked green leaves; 'Yale', red flowers.

Increase all by cuttings, which should dry out for a few hours in the shade before insertion into cutting mix. And raise some from seed. Zone 10.

Petunia

HALF-HARDY ANNUALS Popular summer, windowbox and hanging basket plants, petunias carry their blousy blooms over a long season. Grow in a sunny spot, in good soil or potting mix. Many hybrids are now available, as pot plants or seed, in a very wide range of colors, in single, double and frilled forms as well as picotee and star-patterned bicolors.

In addition to innumerable named single color and bicolored varieties which are readily available, the following mixes will give a good show. 'Bouquet', a formula blend of some nine colors including blue, lilac, red, rose, pink shades and white, large, frilled, double flowers, 12in; 'Dwarf Resisto', medium sized, single flowers noted for their endurance of, and recovery from poor weather conditions, in a wide range of color and some bicolors including shades of violet, blue, rose, scarlet and white, 12in; 'Picotee', large, single, wavy-edged flowers in four colors with white edges, violet, plum, carmine rose and red, 12in.

Raise annually from seed sown indoors in spring. Zones 4–9.

Phormium

SLIGHTLY TENDER EVERGREEN SHRUBS Bold evergreen foliage plants, not fully hardy but doing well in sheltered positions on most patios in all but the worst winters, when the plants should be protected with a covering of straw or leaves. They make striking features set in patio paving spaces or in a suitably large container and require good soil or potting mix and a sunny position.

There are several good garden plants derived from *P. cookianum (P. colensoi)*, the mountain flax and *P. tenax*, the New Zealand flax. They include the following. 'Aurora', bronze leaves striped with red, brown and pink, varies 3–6ft; 'Thumbelina', bronzy purple leaves, only about 12–8in; 'Tricolor', green leaves striped cream and red edged, up to 3ft.

Increase by division in spring. Zone 9.

Picea

HARDY CONIFERS The dwarf spruces provide some fine little evergreens for windowboxes, tubs or patio paving spaces. Grow in good soil or potting mix, in sun or light shade, and provide plenty of water in summer.

There are many good species and their varieties, only a few of which are mentioned here. *P. abies*, the Norway

Below Petunias come in all shades and colors, and are popular for growing in confined areas, such as pots, windowboxes and hanging baskets

spruce, has several interesting forms, such as 'Gregoryana', a dome of gray-green leaves taking many years to reach even 20–24in; 'Nidiformis', a small spreading plant with dark leaves, grows less than 1in a year but eventually may reach up to 3ft high and twice that width. *P. glauca albertiana*, the Alberta spruce, has a few low-growing varieties too, including 'Alberta Globe', a small cylinder of green to about 10in and nearly half as wide; 'Conica', a dense cone only about 3ft high after several years but eventually twice that size and half as wide.

Increase by heeled cuttings taken in early fall. Zones 2–7.

Pinus

HARDY CONIFERS Long needles help to distinguish the pines from the spruces (*Picea*), but otherwise treat and use these dwarf evergreen plants in the same way. A few of the many good plants available are mentioned here.

Pinus densiflora 'Umbraculifera', a small, dense shrub at first, growing about 3ft high and wide after 10 years but eventually forming a fine miniature tree at about 10ft tall and of rather mushroom form. *P. mugo*, the dwarf mountain pine, has many interesting forms including 'Gnom', reaching 20in tall and a bit wider. *P. sylvestris*, the Scots pine, also has a few good dwarf forms, such as 'Beuvronensis', dense growth, taking 10 years or so to reach an eventual 5ft in height and a bit more in width. Zones 2–7.

Primula

HARDY AND HALF-HARDY ANNUALS There are several hundred species of *Primula* but of interest here are the two main groups of popular garden plants, the primroses and polyanthus. They thrive in moist soil or potting mix, and partial shade, in patio beds, window boxes, hanging baskets and indeed virtually any container. There are now many hybrid strains with large and brilliantly colored or bicolored blooms, mainly derived from *P. vulgaris*, the common primrose, and *P. juliae* and crossed with other species.

The polyanthuses are generally taller with a stronger flower stem. Polyanthus hybrid strains include 'Crescendo', hardy

enough to survive outdoors, large flowers in shades of blue, red, pink, yellow and white, 8in; 'Jumbo', scented flowers in shades of blue, red, pink, orange, yellow and white, about 8in; 'New Century', winter hardy, shades of violet blue, crimson, red, orange, yellow and white, tall 12in.

Primrose strains include, 'Cherriette', mixed in shades of purple, red, rose pink, yellow and white, 3–4in; 'Fairy Tale', mixed in shades of blue, carmine, red, pink, yellow and white, scented, 6in.

Besides these mixed strains many single-colored varieties of polyanthus and primrose are available. Sow seed from early spring into summer and increase by dividing clumps in the fall, in mild winter spells and in early spring. Zones 5–8.

Rhododendron

HARDY EVERGREEN SHRUBS Many rhododendrons make good plants for containers provided that they have enough soil to keep their fibrous roots moist and that the soil used is acid. A number of small rhododendrons and azaleas are particularly suitable for patios or windowboxes. Most have the added advantage of being evergreen. If grown in a patio paving space make sure that the soil is non-alkaline or grow in prepared rhododendron mix.

There is a great number of plants to choose from with flowers of most colors except a really true blue. Good varieties include 'Blue Diamond', lavender, small aromatic leaves, reaches 3–5ft;

Above Forming a rounded but open shrub *Rhododendron* 'Baden Baden' with its cherry red trumpet blooms makes an attractive focal point, especially, as shown here, when viewed against a grassed area

'Carmen', blood-red bell shaped flowers, deep green leaves, 12–16in; 'Hinomayo', pink, spreading habit, 5ft, one of the 'Japanese' azaleas; 'Palestrina', white, green-eyed flowers, 2–3ft, another evergreen azalea; 'Praecox', light cerise flowers, very early, semi-evergreen, hardy 3–5ft. *R. yakushimanum* hybrids, in pale to deep pinks, lavender and rose red, very hardy 2–3ft.

Increase by cuttings in summer; these may take a while to root and grow away. Zones 5–9.

Rosa

HARDY DECIDUOUS SHRUBS AND CLIMBERS Roses are very good value as patio plants: most have a long season of flowering, and the different sorts may be put to many uses. There are climbers to grow against the house wall and provide a backdrop for the patio, and others to grow up arbors, pergolas, arches. The ramblers fulfill similar purposes and also scramble over low surrounding walls. There are roses for planting in tubs or to grow as patio hedging, and even miniature kinds for windowboxes and hanging baskets. Roses are found in a huge range of colors. Most appreciate all the sun possible but also do surprisingly well in light shade. Give them a rich moist soil or potting mix and feed them during the growing and flowering season.

When choosing your patio or container

Above Climbing roses such as *Rosa* 'Meg' display flowers from mid summer until late season, while hybrid musks like *Rosa* 'Ballerina' *below* are excellent in borders, having arching stems and close, clustered flowers

roses, think of them on their own merits rather than as belonging to some artificial classification, such as floribunda or hybrid tea. When pruning, bear in mind that hard pruning will most likely induce strong new growths with fewer but larger flowers. Climbers and ramblers may be left more or less to their own devices but ramblers flower mainly on old wood and should be pruned after flowering. Keep all types tidy and within the limits imposed by the site but always cut out diseased or dead wood. The roses described below are given in sections according to their uses and are only a small selection of the many available.

MINIATURE ROSES These are suitable for windowboxes, hanging baskets and other small containers.

BUSH ROSES These varieties are suitable for edging the patio, or as specimens planted in patio paving or in large containers, such as tubs. Make sure that there is good drainage in the containers and stand flat-bottomed containers on tiles or bricks to raise them and allow excess water to drain away; this will also help to delay the rotting of wooden containers. Most of the roses suitable for patios are floribundas (now classed as cluster-flowered bush roses), which are shrubby plants with lots of flowers. The large-flowered bush roses, once known as hybrid teas, are generally too upright and lean of foliage to make good container or specimen plants or to be used for hedging.

CLIMBERS AND RAMBLERS Plant these against walls, pergolas, arches and other structures. Generally speaking no rose is able to climb unless it is growing through a suitable hedge, bush or tree. The so-called climbers, in fact, need to be tied in to other supports, such as trellises, but the ramblers will manage to make a scrambling mound of their own if not given any other support. Zones 4–8.

Salvia

GROWN AS HALF-HARDY ANNUALS Salvias are mainly known for their spectacular scarlet blooms, to which may now be added purple, pink and white varieties. These tender perennials are grown as annuals and are excellent space fillers to provide a splash of color. Grow in sun and good soil or potting mix, in a small patio bed, windowboxes and other containers.

Salvia splendens, scarlet sage, is offered in many varieties including 'Blaze of Fire ('Fireball'), scarlet, early, 12in; 'Dress Parade', a mixed strain including scarlet, pink, purple and white, taller growing 12–14in; 'Laser Purple', deep purple, neat habit 10–12in; 'Red Hot Sally', scarlet, dwarf, useful edging 6–8in.

Raise from seed sown annually in spring indoors. Zones 4–9.

Saxifraga

ROCK PLANTS There are all sorts of saxifrages and some are excellent for decorating low walls, growing in cracks and crevices in the patio or for troughs and even hanging baskets. They must have good drainage and reasonable soil or potting mix. Most appreciate lime.

The mossy hybrids make evergreen cushions and will grow in light shade in wall and paving cracks and crevices. They grow up to 3½–6in tall and about three times that in width. Good varieties include 'Carnival', carmine flowers; 'Flowers of Sulphur', lemon yellow; 'Peter Pan', crimson, low growing. *S. longifolia* has very large spikes of white flowers to about 18in high, over neat rosettes of silvery leaves, the form or hybrid 'Tumbling Waters' has even larger spikes of flower. *S. oppositifolia*, white, pink to crimson flowers over 2-in high mats of leaves spreading to 16in or more, for crevices or troughs, likes a cool, deep, moist root run.

Increase by division in spring. Alternatively, remove offsets in late spring, pot up, and grow on under a cold frame for twelve months. Zone 6.

Scilla

HARDY BULBS One of the squills provides an ideal small, spreading bulb to underplant larger, permanent plantings of shrubs or other perennials, and gives welcome color in late winter or early spring. It will grow in almost any soil or potting mix and in sun or light shade. Good for beds, tubs or other large containers.

Scilla sibirica, the Siberian squill, has nodding flowers of brilliant gentian blue, bright green leaves, 4–6in; a white-flowered form, 'Alba', is also available,

as well as a deeper blue in 'Atrocoerulea' ('Spring Beauty'), which also has slightly larger and earlier flowers.

Increase by division of clumps, offsets and by seed, which is often self-sown. Zones 3–9.

Sedum

ROCK PLANTS Some of the stonecrops may be rather invasive but this may be an advantage if all you can offer are poor soil conditions, such as in a patio crack or dry wall in sun.

There are many species and varieties. *S. acre*, golden-moss stonecrop, star-like yellow flowers in summer, forms evergreen mats of fat, bobbly leaves, to about 2in; very invasive as each broken off leaf is capable of rooting and growing into a plant; the variety 'Aureum' has gold-tipped stems. *S. cauticolum*, rosy crimson flowers, late summer and fall, flat, roundish, blue-gray leaves, deciduous, forms rather loose mats, to 6in. *S. spurium*, pink star flowers in summer, fleshy, flat, evergreen leaves forming large mats, 4–6in high and three to four times as much wide; the form 'Schorbusser Blut' has deep red flowers.

Increase by leaf or stem cuttings. Zones 3–9.

Above Sprays of milky white flowers of *Saxifraga longifolia* 'Tumbling Waters'. Before the blooms appear the plant will form neat leaf rosettes, covering rock or brick surfaces in silvery green cushions

Below The mat-forming evergreen *Sedum acre* looks just as good in a shallow container as in a dry stone wall

Above Dangling stems of *Thunbergia alata* (black-eyed Susan) hang from a basket showing off the plant's orange yellow flowers with their chocolate centers

Right Nasturtiums, like this variety 'Whirlybird Mixed', are adapted for a number of garden purposes, including growing in hanging baskets and windowboxes, and along paths and between rocks and stones

Sempervivum

ROCK PLANTS Excellent crack, crevice and pot plants for sunny spots on a patio, the houseleeks form evergreen rosettes of leaves. Most have pink to red flowers on short, thick stems in summer.

There are masses of species and varieties to choose from. *S. arachnoideum*, cobweb houseleek, rosy red flowers, rosettes of leaves covered with a fine net of white hairs. *S. grandiflorum*, yellow flowers with purple-spotted petals, leaves dull green, brown tipped. *S. marmoreum*, flowers of white-edged crimson petals, green leaves, deep brown tipped; in the variety 'Rubrifolium Ornatum', the leaves are rosy red with green tips. *S. tectorum*, the common houseleek, rosy purple flowers rarely produced, green leaves with deeper tips in several colors according to form, brown, purple or almost violet.

Increase by detaching the new rosettes in early fall and planting them up separately. Zones 4–9.

Tagetes

HALF-HARDY ANNUALS The French and Afro-French marigolds offer bright yellow, orange and mahogany shades of flower. They are super little plants for windowboxes, hanging baskets, edging and space filling around containers with other plants. They appreciate plenty of sun and good soil or potting mix.

Every year the various seed firms offer new strains with double, single, bicolor or self-colored flowers. Height will be between 3–16in according to variety. The French marigolds are derived from *T. patula*, the Afro-French from *T. patula* and *T. erecta*.

Sow annually indoors. Zones 4–9.

Thunbergia

TENDER PERENNIAL CLIMBERS These vines are grown as half-hardy annuals for summer display. They are good, colorful, temporary vines for twining around low supports in windowboxes, pots and other containers, and can also drape from hanging baskets. Grow in any good potting mix, keep moist and feed with liquid fertilizer while growing every ten days or so. Best in sunny and sheltered sites.

Thunbergia alata, black-eyed-Susan, orange-yellow with a chocolate eye, grows up to 10ft; the fine strain 'Susie' has flowers of orange, yellow or white and some with, others without, a dark eye, to 4ft. *T. fragrans* 'Angel Wings', has larger, lightly fragrant, yellow-eyed white flowers.

Sow seed annually in spring indoors. Zones 8–10.

Tropaeolum

HARDY ANNUALS AND PERENNIALS The nasturtiums include plants for all sorts of situations, perennial and annual vines, as well as the familiar annually raised garden nasturtium. Grow in sun or partial shade in fairly reasonable soil or potting mix.

Tropaeolum majus, common garden nasturtium, flowers in various shades of crimson, red, orange, yellow and cream, and is now available in three forms. 1. Compact, dwarf, bushy plants suitable for all containers and including 'Alaska', mixed colors, with variegated leaves, eye-catching 8in; 'Fiery Festival', mixed colors, fragrant, 6in; and in named colors such as 'Peach Melba', creamy yellow with scarlet blotches. 2. Semi-trailing, compact varieties, excellent for trailing from hanging baskets or other containers, including 'Gleam', mixed colors, with double blooms, also some colors available separately, about 12in. 3. Climbing or trailing varieties which need to be tied in to a support if used for climbing, and usually available only as single blooms in mixed colors.

Tropaeolum peltophorum (T. lobbianum) is an annual vine with orange and red flowers, grows to 5–6ft. *T. peregrinum (T. canariense)*, Canary creeper, annual vine with bright fringed yellow flowers, to 13ft. *T. speciosum*, flame creeper, a nearly hardy climbing herbaceous perennial with scarlet flowers which does best in cool places, such as against a partially sunny house wall. Grows 6–10ft high.

Raise annuals by seed, and increase the flame creeper by division. Zones 4–9.

Tulipa

HARDY BULBS Almost all tulips may be grown in containers and the choice, therefore, must be made to fit the situation and type of container. Tall tulips will be less likely to remain upright in windy weather and generally are best avoided, especially in windowboxes or containers exposed to wind. Many of the dwarfer sorts are excellent in such situations and they are often much easier to grow too. Plant in a sunny spot and use potting mix in the container. Lift the bulbs when the leaves have turned yellow. Replant each fall.

Only a few of the many possible tulips are given here. Double early hybrids have very double flowers in a good range of colors, they grow to about 10–14in, and include 'Orange Nassau', orange shaded brown; 'Schoonoord' ('Purity'), bright white. Greigii hybrids come in a wide variety of colors, and often have wavy leaves, striped or mottled with brownish marks, and grow from 6–16in tall, varieties include 'Cape Cod', yellow shaded bronze and apricot and with a red stripe and 'Peacock', a mixture which includes lavender and red shades. Kaufmanniana hybrids, sometimes called waterlily tulips, have large, flattish, starry flowers, many with striped or mottled leaves, these grow 5–8in high and include 'Hearts Delight', rose exterior, creamy yellow interior blotched red, and 'Shakespeare', salmon, apricot and yellow. Single early, single blooms in a wide variety of colors, mainly in the range 6–16in, including 'Brilliant Star', scarlet, black and yellow; 'Diana', white. Other hybrid groups are generally much taller growing.

Increase by offsets. Zones 4–8.

Vitis

HARDY DECIDUOUS CLIMBERS The grapes include some attractively colored-leaf varieties, some of which appear under grapes on page 77. The grape described here is a purely ornamental climber. It may be grown over large structures or into a trellis, and needs sun and good soil. *V. coignetiae*, crimson glory vine, has large, roundish, lobed leaves, up to 8in across, which turn rich colors in the fall, grows to 65½–82ft.

Increase by eye cuttings. Zones 5–8.

Wisteria

HARDY DECIDUOUS CLIMBER A wonderful vine for clothing a wall, framing doors and windows, growing over an arched trellis, or planted on its own as a magnificent weeping specimen to make a patio centre-piece. When wall grown the twining stems will need support from wires or trellis. Grow in a sunny place in good soil, allowing plenty of room for root growth.

Wisteria floribunda, Japanese wisteria, with flowers in various shades of violet, lilac, pink and white, and often well scented is the best for trellis or specimen uses; varieties include 'Alba', white tinged lilac; 'Macrobotrys' (*W. multijuga*), violet to lilac-purple in long clusters; 'Rosea', pink; 'Violacea Plena', violet-blue, double. *W. sinensis*, Chinese wisteria, with flowers in similar shades, is the best for wall support, varieties include 'Alba', white; 'Black Dragon', dark purple, double.

Increase by cuttings in early fall. Zones 5–8.

Below A cascading profusion of light, violet blue wisteria panicles illustrates that this vine will provide a dense clothing over a wall — or a pergola. Hard pruning encourages a good spread of blooms

CHAPTER SIX

FRUIT FOR THE PATIO

Opposite The Victoria plum, suitably fed and trained to allow the sun to reach all parts of the tree, will provide large quantities of fruit, being an almost self-fertile plant

Below Pears, like this variety 'Packhams Triumph', are very adaptable to being trained as cordons, a space saving method which will provide attractive spring blossom along a fence or wall

PATIOS ARE A GOOD place to grow some of the popular fruits. The environment created by a wall and paving is likely to be warmer than in the open garden, the heat of the sun being radiated onto and improving the ripening of fruit. The drainage is usually good, too. Fruit picked at the right time, ripe and lusciously juicy, is so superior to most bought fruit, which has to be picked unripe if it is to travel well, that it is as a new taste experience. Weeding, fertilizing and control of pests and diseases is much easier than in a garden too. Described here are a few of the fruits which should do well, and it really is worth trying anything else you fancy.

Fruit Growing in Containers

Many of the fruits will crop well when they are grown in containers. Fertilizing, watering and aftercare follows the same general rules given earlier for ornamental plants. It is best to use a heavy soil-based potting mix and to repot as the plants grow and fill their pots with roots. Of the fruits recommended for pot culture, gooseberries and grapes will need potting on until a pot size of 1½–1¾ gallon (9–10in) is reached, a fig will need a half tub and strawberries may be grown in almost any size or type of container, from about ½ gallon (6in) for one plant to half tubs containing seven or eight plants spaced from 6–12in apart according to the tub size. Special purpose pots are particularly useful.

Pruning and training

Pruning will need some care, as will training where this is necessary. Pruning consists of removing diseased and damaged wood as well as cutting out some shoots to stimulate the production of fruiting spurs or branches. Once the tree or shrub is trained it should be possible to keep it in production for many years with light pruning only. The typical forms or shapes used for growing fruit against walls are espalier, cordon and fan.

ESPALIER An espalier is an upright tree with regularly spaced pairs of side branches trained at right angles from the main trunk or stem. The side branches are tied to horizontal wires, stretched

between posts or against a wall. It is a good way to train pears and grapes over pergolas too.

In the pear the horizontal branches are spaced about 15–18in apart. Any number of tiers may be developed but four or five is usual and to save time trees may be bought with two or three tiers already formed. In the case of grapes, about 18–20in is allowed between each tier. The wider spacing makes for easy picking.

Tie the pear branches to their supporting wires and cut back the leading growth of each by about a quarter, making the cut to an upward-facing bud. The central stem should be cut back to a bud about 2in above the next wire. Below this bud, choose a bud on either side of the stem to grow on as the new branches, rubbing out all other buds to prevent them developing too. Do this annually until enough tiers have been formed, then, for the final tier, cut the main stem just above the topmost of the two selected branch buds.

Prune all the side branches in late summer, cutting them back to one leaf above the basal cluster of the new growth. Only if excessive growth due to a wet summer occurs, should further pruning be necessary later in the season. Repeat the summer pruning annually.

When training the two side branches start them off at an angle of 45 degrees, then note their growth rate and lower or raise the branches to stimulate or depress growth (raising stimulates, lowering depresses) until the branches are matched in length.

CORDONS These are single stem forms, usually grown at an angle of about 45 degrees, from which short, fruiting branches or spurs are developed. Upright cordons are another possibility but these take up a bit more space for a given fruiting length of stem. Whatever angle is used, the main stem or trunk must be tied in for support and training. Prune in summer as for espaliers. This is a good form where space for growing pears, gooseberries and grapes is limited.

FANS This is an excellent method of training plums, morello cherries, gooseberries and pears against a wall. The basic formation is made from two branches which are allowed to form the main support growth, the central leader being removed. The two branches are successively pruned until each supports four branches. In the third winter, each of these branches is cut back to about 22in, making the cut just above a bud. Keep tying the branches in to evenly spaced canes, which themselves are tied to horizontal wires. Allow three further buds to develop on each branch; these will give rise to twenty-four new ribs, making a total of thirty-two. Remove other unwanted shoots.

Once the thirty-two ribs are mature, remove the canes and tie the ribs directly to the wires. From then on summer prune as for espaliers, and in winter prune away any unwanted shoots.

Cherry

Cherries might be thought of only in terms of large trees, but there are two varieties, both self fertile and so suitable for growing on their own, which will make admirable plants for a patio. They need a well limed, potash-rich fertile soil. The morello cherry is a superb wall plant when trained as a fan. The wall may be north facing, too, and the minimum height required is about 10ft. The fruit is dark crimson and is the best for preserves, tarts and other culinary purposes, including making cherry brandy.

'Stella' is a sweet cherry with blackish-red dessert fruit. It makes a fine upright tree and is worth trying if you have a large patio, perhaps at the side where a bed might be made for it. Make sure to get it on the semi-dwarfing rootstock 'Colt' or you may well have a problem with its growth. Stella fruits from mid to late summer. Net the fruits, or the birds will probably get them first. Keep well watered or fruits may split.

Below Gooseberries can be trained into fans, standards and cordons, saving space on a patio and allowing easier access to the fruit

Right The sour cherry, Morello, whose fruit is used for preserves, will tolerate a north facing wall, and look as attractive there as an ornamental shrub

Fig

A freshly picked, sun-ripened fig is a memorable taste experience. Fig trees make very decorative foliage plants, too, with their deeply lobed leaves and are ideal when grown against a wall. The fig must have a warm, sheltered position if it is to produce good fruit. In addition to being grown in a prepared bed against the wall, they will grow well in large pots or other containers. Indeed root restriction is essential for good fruit production. Avoid over fertilizing.

To prepare a bed against a wall, dig a hole about 3ft square and as deep, and line it with bricks or concrete, leaving it open at the bottom. Fill in with brick rubble or gravel to a depth of 12in and top this with a good loamy soil to which has been added a little rubble. Good loam mixed with some fine brick rubble is also suitable for filling containers, which must have a good drainage.

Figs may also be trained as fans but take care not to remove the young developing fruit which requires two seasons to mature. The fig produces two flushes of fruit, one in spring which may be removed as in a cool climate it will not mature — these fruits are formed in the leaf axils. The second flush is borne in late summer at the shoot tips and, if all else is well, this will mature the next summer, so it is important not to cut these off.

Good varieties are 'Brown Turkey', brownish-red fruit covered with a bloom, the heaviest cropper, mid-season, good against walls; 'Brunswick', brownish yellow green fruit, early mid-season; 'White Marseilles', green tinged white fruit, translucent when ripe, sweet, mid-season, good as bush.

Gooseberry

Gooseberries, although enjoying some sun, are also adaptable for the less sunny patio corners. Grow them either in a patio paving space, large pot or other container. While several plants are needed to provide large crops for cooking, for dessert purposes one or two will give an acceptable quantity of fruit. Gooseberries are host to a serious disease of pines and are prohibited in some areas.

Gooseberries need a well drained soil or potting mix and may be grown in a variety of ways apart from the usual

bush, they may be trained as a fan, cordon or standard and the fruit is then much easier to pick.

Add plenty of well rotted organic amendment to the soil before planting.

The varieties described are all recommended for dessert fruit. 'Broomgirl', deliciously flavored, early, yellow, spreading bush; 'Early Sulphur', very good flavor, very early, yellow, upright bush; 'Langley Gage', very good flavor, mid season, greenish white, upright bush; 'Whinham's Industry', good flavor, sweet, mid season, red, spreading to upright bush good in partial shade, also culinary use. Heavy yielding.

Grape

While grape vines may be grown in a variety of situations they need warmth. Grow them against a wall, over a low wall, pergola or arch, from a bed in the patio paving or a large container. They may even be trained as standards. The grapes described here are mainly for dessert, though wine may also be made from them; wine grapes are really another subject.

The best grapes will be obtained from plants grown against a sunny wall, in well drained soil enriched with good, rotted manure or organic amendment. Plant in winter or early spring. Train wall grown grapes as single or double cordons and make sure that they do not suffer from dryness.

Above Despite the fact that they are normally regarded as trees, figs can be grown in large containers since restriction of the roots encourages the formation of fruit

Right The grape, *Vitis vinifera*, is a hardy deciduous climber, needing plenty of sun in the summer for fruit setting. This variety, 'Madeleine Angevine', is a vigorous white grape maturing in the early fall

Besides the cordon form, grapes may be trained along a single or double stem, selecting the strongest shoot and pruning it back to a bud in early winter. Cut back all side shoots to the two buds near the shoot base. Let the main shoot grow each year and cut it back as described until the required length is achieved. Regular pruning is then needed to keep the plant fruitful. Thin out the lateral shoots when the flowers appear, allowing one shoot to each spur with a spacing of about 10in between each, keeping only those with the best flower bunches. Cut back unwanted shoots to one leaf; then pinch out the remaining shoots two or three leaves beyond the flower bunch. If any further side shoots form cut them down to one leaf too. In early winter after the leaves have fallen, cut back the previous year's shoots to a fat bud, leaving one or two buds only to sprout the next season. Do not let young vines bear too many bunches of grapes as this will ruin flavor and quality. A three-year-old vine may be allowed to carry only two or three bunches, a four-year-old only four or five, and so on until a mature vine is able to support a bunch every 6in or so. Thinning outdoor grapes is not usually carried out as most of the suitable varieties produce small grapes.

Good varieties include 'Brant', usually listed as 'Brandt', early, small, sweet, black grapes, the most reliable cropper, attractive in the fall when the leaves color well; 'Chasselas Doré de Fontainbleu', usually listed as 'Royal Muscadine', early, medium, sweet, white, with some muscat flavor, good as a wall grown cordon; 'Miller's Burgundy', also known as 'Dusty Miller' because of the downy leaves, small to medium, sweet, black grapes; 'Siegerrebe', medium, early, brown grapes, also suitable for wine.

Pear

Perfect pears cannot be bought; you have to grow them yourself and a wall backing a patio is a perfect place. Most varieties in the stores are there because they are reasonably hard and travel well but they are, at best, only reasonably flavored. With the exception of 'Conference', the varieties described here have mouth-watering fruit. 'Conference' is included because it is very easy to grow and not completely reliant on other pollinators to produce a crop, though it is a useful pollinator itself.

These superb varieties may be grown on walls, trained as fans, cordons or espaliers. If not wall trained, try trees trained as dwarf pyramids, about 6½–8ft high, in patio paving beds. Plant in good soil, digging in organic soil amendment or manure if possible, and adding a little balanced fertilizer just before planting. A neutral to only slight acid soil is best and good drainage is essential.

To ensure a crop another pear which flowers at the same time must be grown nearby. In the list of varieties, those flowering at the same time are indicated by a 2, 3 or 4 after their names. 'Beurré Superfin', 3, excellent quality, red-flushed russet and yellow; 'Conference', 3, will produce fruit without pollination but bigger crops with, russet, greenish yellow; 'Doyenné du Comice', 4, superb, red-flushed yellow; 'Durondeau', 3, juicy, compact growing, red-flushed yellow and russet; 'Emile d'Heyst', 2, luscious, yellowish green reliable; 'Glou Morceau', 4, delicious, greenish yellow and russet, for a warm and sheltered position; 'Joséphine de Malines', 3, delicious, greenish yellow, good crops but not a strong grower; 'Louise Bonne of Jersey', 2, superb, red-flushed yellowish green.

Plum

Superb fruit when picked ripe for immediate eating: unobtainable at this stage in the shops. There are several varieties well worth trying on a patio, some for a wall and some as free standing, small trees. A patio is especially good for some of the more tender varieties, such as the gages.

Plums may be grown as standards, half standards, or trained as fans against a wall. They need a good soil, moisture retentive and slightly alkaline. Add

Left This strawberry variety is 'Gento' one of the remontant types which will give sweet fruit at intervals from June to October. Single plants raised in pots will often produce larger fruit than strawberries grown in rows with their runners left intact

plenty of organic soil amendment or manure before planting and mulch with additional material after planting. Feed annually with a high nitrogen fertilizer, or a balanced fertilizer plus additional nitrogen. Keep moist in the growing season.

The dessert varieties listed here are self-fertile unless otherwise described. 'Denniston's Superb', a medium early, greengage; 'Early Transparent Gage', a mid season gage of superb flavor and juicyness, red spots on yellow, a compact, small tree; 'Kirke's', medium late, excellent flavor, purple with a bluish bloom, needs a pollinator such as 'Early Transparent Gage', small tree, needs a warm site; 'Victoria', a very popular plum, red and yellow, of fair flavor, almost completely self-fertile, prolific and best against a wall.

Quince

Ornamental in flower and foliage and with fragrant fruit, the quince is truly an all purpose shrub. Use it as a surrounding hedge or trained against a patio wall as a fan. Grow in good soil and in the sunniest spot. 'Portugal' makes a good specimen shrub but is slow to produce its mild flavored yellow fruit; 'Vranja' is excellent for a wall and has large yellow fruit of good flavor.

Strawberry

This fruit is suitable for any container, tub, pot, urn, special strawberry planter, as well as patio beds, hanging baskets and windowboxes. Strawberries are short lived as productive plants, and you must be prepared to grow replacement plants or buy them in as necessary. A good, well drained soil or potting mix, acid rather than alkaline, and a sunny site, are preferred. When preparing the bed, mix plenty of organic matter into the soil.

There are three main types of strawberry grown, summer fruiting and remontant (perpetual) fruiting types, and also alpine strawberries. Some people prefer to remove the flowers of summer-fruiting varieties in their first year after planting in the hope of a bigger crop the following year. The summer-fruiting types usually have a productive life of three years, the remontants of two years, while the alpines die out quite quickly to be continuously replaced by new self-sown seedlings. The alpines have the best flavor, the larger summer and remontant fruiting types are often sweeter and juicier. Sow seed of alpines in spring or in the fall, plant summer and remontant fruiters in summer.

Recommended varieties include 'Alexandria', delicious flavored, red fruited alpine; 'Alpine Yellow', 'Pineapple Crush' and 'Yellow Wonder', appear to be very similar, yellowish white fruited alpines of excellent flavor; 'Gento', a remontant variety, good crops of medium sized, sweet fruit; 'Grandee', a summer variety, very large and very sweet fruit; 'Royal Sovereign', a summer variety, aromatic and juicy; 'Sweetheart', summer fruiting, sweet, medium sized fruit, easily raised from seed; 'Tonto', summer fruiting, large crops of medium sized, well flavored fruit.

CHAPTER SEVEN

VEGETABLES AND HERBS

Right Herbs are an excellent choice for both patio and windowbox. As shown here, a mixture of the commonest, mint, parsley and thyme, planted in a selection of terracotta pots will provide attractive as well as edible foliage

IT IS TRUE that you are very unlikely to become anywhere near self-sufficient by growing vegetables on a patio, let alone in a windowbox. You will, however, be able to grow quite a few vegetables, especially salad ones, very well. Careful selection of varieties can give fine crops through the summer and fall, less in winter or spring. Moreover, if you confine your planting to containers, tubs pots, buckets, urns, growing bags and windowboxes, for instance, you will most likely avoid most of the pests and diseases, and weeds too, which afflict soil-grown vegetables.

Sowing seed

Obviously the usual vegetable garden practice of planting or sowing in rows needs revision according to what you are growing. As containers are comparatively small compared to gardens, it becomes even more worthwhile to space seed individually, and this is not as difficult as it may sound. An exception to this is a crop like carrots, which is marvellous if broadcast sown in a tub.

Seed of some vegetables — courgettes, celery, sweet peppers and tomatoes, for example — should be sown under cover as described for ornamental plants, p.30. In the case of very large seeds, such as courgettes, sow individually in small 3in pots; some people recommend sowing two seeds to each pot and removing the weaker seedling if they both germinate. I prefer to sow an extra pot or two to make up any loss. Tomatoes and sweet peppers may also be sown individually in small pots and grown on without disturbance before planting out in a growing bag or other container.

Growing bags

The actual number of plants which may be grown in a growing bag depends on the producer. Most growing bags will take three or four tomato plants, three peppers, two courgettes, ten beans and so on: read the instructions given by the manufacturer of your particular bag. For unmentioned vegetables it is a matter of experiment but, generally speaking, you will be able to grow more vegetables in the space of a growing bag than that recommended for a similar soil area, just decrease the normal planting distance slightly.

Beans

Beans are a versatile and easily grown crop for containers and patio paving spaces. Snap or string beans are the most generally cultivated and there are both bush and climbing varieties. This is a frost tender crop, so do not plant out until danger of frost is past and the soil has started to warm up.

The best container is a half tub of about 28–32in diameter. Fill it with good well draining potting mix after placing it in a sunny spot. Sow dwarf beans individually, about 5in apart in all directions, in late spring. For climbers make a wigwam of 6½ft bamboos; tie them firmly together at the top and sow individual beans at their bases. You should be able to get 6–8 beans to each tub so it is worth choosing heavy croppers.

Good bush varieties include 'Tendergreen', 'Pencil Pod', 'Tendercrop' and 'Jumbo', which has large, flat green pods of good flavour. 'Royalty' or 'Royal Burgundy' have purple pods of excellent flavour. For climbers try 'Blue

Lake', 'Kentucky Wonder' or 'White Creaseback'.

Beets

Beets may be grown in large containers, including tubs and growing bags. Due to the restricted space available it is worth getting as much of a crop as possible so choose a cylindrical variety rather than a round one. Either use fresh potting mix or sow directly into soil used the previous year for beans. Choose a position in sun or light shade. Feed occasionally with a low nitrogen fertilizer during the growing season.

One of the best cylindrical beets is 'Forono'; this will grow up to 3in or more long and about half as wide. Space individual seed clusters about 3in apart in all directions and thin each cluster to one plant when they have germinated.

Carrot

Excellent tub growers, substantial crops may be achieved from a barrel 28in, or more, in diameter, lesser crops from smaller containers. Place in a sunny or light shaded area. The round, short rooted carrots are a complete waste of time, giving little to eat and that of only fair flavour. Short cylindrical rooted are good in the shallower containers, longer rooted types in tubs and any other deep container.

Use fresh soil or that previously used to raise beans and add insecticide before sowing to discourage root flies. Sow broadcast. The first thinnings will provide delicious little carrots for salads or adding whole to cooked peas. Continue thinning from all over the area sown, so that eventually you end up with good sized carrots.

Right Short cylindrical rooted carrots can be raised in growing bags provided that they have plenty of nutrients in the form of a balanced potting mix

Good varieties include 'Asmer Babycan', which is suitable for all types of container; 'Camus', 'Mokum', and 'Nantes', are good in all but the smallest containers.

Celery

A good vegetable for half tubs, the self-blanching celery, may also be grown in growing bags. In tubs filled to within 4–6in of the rim, the sides provide useful support; fresh potting mix, or soil used previously for beans, should be used. Before sowing or planting hand fork in soil insecticide to deter root flies. Sow or plant about 6in apart in all directions; closer spacing will give more plants but with thinner sticks. Keep moist. Good varieties are 'Celebrity', 'Golden Self Blanching' and 'Ivory Tower'.

Courgette

Courgettes will grow rampantly from half tubs or growing bags. Use fresh potting mix, or soil previously used to raise beans. Choose a sunny place. Sow or plant two courgettes a couple of inches apart in the centre of a 28-in diameter tub, or three equally spaced in a circle 6–8in in from the sides. In growing bags use two plants unless the labels advise otherwise. Keep well watered.

There are a number of good varieties. The bush types are the most suitable and these include 'Blondy', delicious, firm flesh, pale green skin, early and heavy cropping; 'Burpee Golden Zucchini', butter yellow slim fruits; 'Gold Rush', a fine yellow-skinned variety; 'Zucchini', a favorite heavy cropping variety, with excellent flavored, long green fruit.

Lettuce

First class lettuce may be grown in containers, especially tubs and growing bags as well as windowboxes and any pot that is large enough. Indeed the best flavored lettuces, small, sweet and succulent will thrive; so will larger crisphead types but they will taste, if they have a flavor at all, similar to shop bought ones. It is often more convenient to have a few small lettuces rather than a large one.

Grow in fresh soil or that previously used for beans, in sun or light shade. Feed with a high nitrogen fertilizer during the growing season. Sow several times at intervals of a fortnight or so for successional crops, or sow too many and transplant some of the seedlings; the transplanted lettuces will be slower to mature than those left undisturbed. Spacing will depend on variety, but small lettuces may be grown at only 4in apart at first and using every other one so that those remaining are gradually allowed more space; large lettuces may be spaced at 5in so that after alternate thinning there is space of about 10in between the remaining plants.

Good lettuces to grow like this include 'Little Gem' ('Sugar Cos'), a variable variety, sometimes more cos than cabbage, or the reverse, but always small and compact, dark green with good flavoured leaves; 'Tom Thumb', a splendid small crisp cabbage, hard to fault, sweet, excellently flavored, medium green leaves; 'Webbs Wonderful', seemingly still unsurpassed for a large, crisp leaved lettuce and a reliable crop.

Radish

A crop which will grow in any container with enough soil or potting mix; you might even try them in a hanging basket. Use fresh mix or that used previously for beans. Sow successively from late spring onwards. Keep moist and place the container in a lightly or partially shaded spot. Before sowing add insecticide to the soil as a preventive against root fly attack.

Choose varieties according to the depth of soil available, globe sorts for the shallowest containers, long-rooted ones for the deepest. Good varieties are 'French Breakfast' with cylindrical roots, usually red with white tips; 'Prinz Rotin' ('Red Prince'), the finest globe and capable of growing very large before deteriorating; 'Long White Icicle', an excellent long white radish.

Squash

Squashes, and especially the summer cropping varieties, make a good crop for warm climates. Choose one of the bush forms for growing in a large container, growing bag or patio paving space in a sunny position. Use a good potting mix or soil to which organic matter has been added.

In cooler areas plant out when danger of frost is past. In warmer areas seeds can be sown outdoors when the soil has warmed up. Sow seeds two inches apart, two or three to a container.

Keep plants well watered and fertilize regularly as soon as the young fruits are visible.

Harvest while the rinds are soft — try piercing them with your fingernail.

Good varieties include 'Bush Scallop' and 'Early Prolific Straightneck'.

Sweet pepper

Fine peppers may be grown in pots and growing bags, or indeed any other large enough container. Allow three peppers to each growing bag and one to a 8in pot. Unfortunately there are a number of peppers which are hardly worth growing, giving poor main crops of thin walled fruit, but those recommended below are of good quality, one is thin walled but still worth growing.

Use any good potting mix for pot grown plants. Keep peppers moist and feed them every ten days beginning as the fruits start to swell, with a liquid tomato fertilizer. Stake the plants to prevent them toppling over. 'Golden Bell', yellow, thick walled, may be sown directly outside, mid season; 'Gold Star',

Below If space is at a minimum radishes are a wise choice for a home grown vegetable. Planted at intervals they will give a continuous supply of roots throughout the summer

yellow, thick walled, mid to late season; both these for about 8in pots. 'Triton', red, thin walled but very early, sweet, crisp fruit, which appears in clusters at the top of the plants, outstanding, for 6in pots.

Tomato

There can be no doubt that the best way to grow tomatoes on a patio is in growing bags. These overcome the disadvantages and diseases of soil-grown plants and get rid of the messiness of pot culture. A few dwarf varieties of tomato have appeared in recent years, reputedly producing good tomatoes in small, 5in pots; they are poor eating but decorative. You can grow tomatoes of superlative quality, however, in growing bags backed against a wall for extra warmth. Keep moist and feed with liquid fertilizer as directed on the bag or fertilizer container. Support for tomatoes grown in bags against a wall is easily provided by canes or hooks secured to the wall or windowsill. Otherwise special wire frames for the bags are available. Bush forms will not need this, of course, but may benefit from having straw placed between the hanging trusses and the patio floor.

Tomatoes grown up canes will need regular pinching out: that is removing all side shoots which develop at leaf and main stem joints. This is continued until four or five trusses of flower have started to set tomatoes. Then pinch out the top of the main stem to stop further development. The truss shoots appear directly from the main stem and not from the leaf

joints and so are easily distinguished. With bush tomatoes no pinching out is needed.

Which variety to grow will depend to some extent on personal preferences for some people choose by size rather than flavour. 'Gardeners Delight', masses of small fruit, sweet juicy, red and of outstanding flavor, tall; 'Golden Sunrise', good sized golden fruit of delicious flavor, not acid, tall; 'Pixie', lots of small to medium tomatoes, reasonable flavor, bush; 'Red Alert', small fruit of fair flavor but early, bush; 'Super Marmande', large ribbed fruit, red, good flavor, tall; 'Sweet 100', strings of small, very sweet, red fruit.

HERBS

There are few herbs that will not do well grown on or in a patio; many will also perform well in windowboxes and some in hanging baskets too. They will all accept containers of the right size for the plants concerned and for rapid spreaders, such as the mints, it is sometimes a good thing that they are so confined.

Herb associations

Herbs also associate well in mixed plantings and should be treated just as you would ornamental plants. Place the taller growing ones towards the center of an arrangement, rosemary or common marjoram for instance, and surround these with the lower growing thymes, basil or chives. The edges can be planted with the sprawling sweet marjoram or a creeping thyme. It is best, however, to keep the more rampant spreading herbs to themselves or you will have considerable problems in disentangling mints for example, or even tarragon, from other plants. Sage, too, is a bit of a nuisance in this respect and is apt to sprawl rather heavily and so suppress other, lower growing plants in the vicinity.

If you have very large containers it is worth considering perhaps three planting schemes, a shrubby one of bay, rosemary, winter savory and thyme, for instance, a perennial one of tarragon, common marjoram and chives, and an annual scheme of summer savory, basil and sweet marjoram. Herbs which accept hanging baskets are mentioned under the individual herb descriptions.

Below Lined up against the railings of this balcony these tomatoes, planted two to each growbag are in a good position for fruit ripening, and also for providing a welcome green barrier in an urban setting

Preserving herbs

The easiest way of drying herbs is to pick the shoots when dry and in full leaf but preferably before they flower. Without mixing up the herbs, tie the bunches near the stem ends and hang them upside down in an airy, warm and dry place. In a week or two, the dried leaves can be stripped from the stems. This can be done more quickly in the oven. Lay individual stems of leaves on greaseproof paper in a low oven for a few hours, and with the oven door slightly ajar, until they are dry. Some people recommend stripping the leaves first for this method, and it does save a little time, simply place the individual leaves on the greaseproof paper and treat as above. Store in airtight jars.

Another way of preserving herbs is to freeze them. The two best methods are to freeze small bunches of unblanched herbs and then to place them in containers in the freezer. Alternatively, wrap chopped herbs in foil and freeze.

The following list includes the main culinary herbs. If there is some other herb that you fancy but which is not included, do try it, most are very easy to grow.

Basil

A superbly flavored annual herb, wonderful with tomato and salad dishes, soups, stews and drinks. It must be started indoors and then only become a patio, or windowbox inhabitant, during the warmest months. Plant in good soil, in pots which may be disguised in other containers, such as urns, windowboxes or hanging baskets. Keep moist and feed while growing in summer and early fall. Keep plants bushy by pinching out the growing tip, and, when cropping, work downwards to induce more branching — picking off individual leaves will produce straggly, weak plants. Grow in a sunny, warm spot.

There are two main forms grown. Sweet basil has larger and better flavored leaves than bush basil, but one smaller leafed form, 'Green Bouquet', is of good flavor too.

Bay

An excellent evergreen patio shrub, grows well in tubs and other large containers. Accepts clipping, and pairs of clipped bay look good flanking doors on to patios or by patio steps. If you can spare a patio paving space, then plant your bay to get the best bush. Bay will grow in well drained soil or potting mix and in sun or partial shade, but it does not respond well to winter wet or too cold a spot.

Chervil

Wonderful with egg dishes and adds interest to salads, chicken and stews. It makes a tall plant, up to 4ft, if given good soil and a position that it likes, but is usually about 1½ft and looks like a large, pale but bright green parsley. Grow in pots or tubs or use to underplant small shrubs or trees, in sun or partial shade. Sow annually.

Chives

Easily grown in almost any soil or potting mix, perennial chives will do best in reasonably good, well drained moist soil in partial shade. Plant in paving spaces, as underplanting or on its own, in

Above Slightly more informal than most potted bays this specimen has a rustic home in a wooden half-barrel tub

Above An unusual tower pot used for growing mints, sage, parsley, and chives. Made up of modular units, the single pots can be bought and assembled in the numbers you require

windowboxes, pots and even hanging baskets. Feed with liquid fertilizer occasionally during the summer. Divide the clumps every few years and replant as required for rejuvenation. Apart from the usual uses for the leaves, the opening flower heads make a tasty and attractive addition to soups and salads. Chives may be bought as small clumps or started from seed. Anyone not growing a few clumps is missing out.

Coriander

This herb is gaining favor due to its use in Chinese and Mexican dishes, now popular in modern cooking. It is a graceful annual plant, with attractive, very fine, dark green ferny leaves. They are good used in salads, stews and curries. The seeds, which have a different flavor, are also used in many Indian dishes. Grow in pots or windowboxes, plant in potting mix and keep moist, and place in a sunny, warm position. Raise annually from seed.

Fennel

A tall perennial, often grown annually for its finely divided leaves which have a rather tarry aniseed flavor, and reaching a height of 2–4ft. It is good with fish and salads. Grow as an accent to fill a patio paving space or in a fairly large container. The seeds are also used in Oriental cooking and indeed, once a plant is grown, plenty of self sown seedlings will usually appear in following years. The bronze leaved form is of similar flavor to the green, and both are raised annually from seed.

Marjoram

Roasts, grills, pizzas, and many summer drinks may benefit from the addition of one or other of the marjorams. Best known is probably common marjoram or oregano, which is much used in Italian cooking, followed by the better flavored sweet or knotted marjoram, useful in salads, with tomatoes, in cooked dishes and as a flavoring for drinks. Both are perennial, sweet marjoram is usually grown as an annual and should be treated as described for sweet basil, it reaches a height of about 8–12in. Common marjoram accepts a role in a border flanking the patio or on its own in a

container; it grows 24–28in. Plant in reasonably good soil or potting mix and in a sunny spot. Both are easily raised from seed.

Mint

There are many mints, some are very good culinary plants, others definitely not so good for such things as mint sauce. The three described here are all good container plants, but not for hanging baskets, however. Grow in good moist soil or potting mix in a sunny or lightly shaded spot.

Apple or round leaved mint is a delightful plant with light green, woolly leaves of exceptional flavor, which grows about 2ft. French or Bowles mint has larger woolly leaves than apple mint, grows taller to 2½–4ft and is stronger flavored. Spearmint is quite different with willow-like leaves and is probably the most readily available mint; it has a sharper and coarser flavor than the other two mints and is liable to be attacked by rust; it grows about 1½–3ft. The roots of all these mints will rapidly fill containers, and plants should be divided up, every other year or so in spring, and small portions replanted.

Parsley

A favorite food garnish in Britain but used elsewhere as an essential flavoring for sauces and in stews. Curly leaved and flavorsome plain leaved forms are readily obtainable. Grow in pots, window boxes, or other containers, or in patio beds and as an underplanting. Self-sown seedlings usually keep plants going from year to year but to be safe, as parsley is biennial, raise a few new plants annually. Parsley seed is rather slow and irregular in germination.

Rosemary

A fine evergreen shrub with lilac flowers in spring. The leaves provide a superb flavoring for lamb and chicken and are also used in drinks. Pieces scattered on a barbecue scent the air. Grow as an accent plant in a patio paving space, or in a large container and in a sunny or lightly shaded, sheltered spot. Plant in good, well drained soil or potting mix. There are various forms available with different flower shades or slightly different growth habits, but the leaf flavor is similar. Increase by cuttings.

Sage

A sprawling, evergreen shrubby plant, sage is a famous flavoring in sausages and stuffings. It will add considerably to stews and summer drinks too. The grayish green leaves are strongly aromatic but some of the colored leaved forms less so. Grow in sun in beds, containers and windowboxes. Keep plants trimmed or they will get very straggly. Most forms grow about 1–2ft tall.

Salvia officinalis, common sage, is the best culinary form and the hardiest garden plant. There are some colored leaved varieties which are decorative for a while but usually become rather straggly and they are not as hardy as the common sage, sometimes not surviving over winter. 'Icterina' has yellow-edged leaves; 'Purpurascens' has leaves tinged with purple; 'Tricolor' gray, cream, pink and purplish leaves.

Increase all kinds by cuttings or layering.

Savory

The two forms of savory grown are very different plants but are used in the same way. Summer savory is an annual and has a slightly better flavor than winter savory; it grows about 8–12in tall. Winter savory is an evergreen shrubby plant and so is available all the year round; it also grows 8–12in tall but is a small spreading bush.

Use both for flavoring stews and other meat and vegetable dishes. Savory is particularly recommended as an addition to beans. Grow summer savory as for sweet basil but plant winter savory in some permanent position, such as a patio paving space or crevices in paving, or as an edging or in a windowbox. It needs sun and well drained conditions. Sow summer savory annually; increase winter savory by cuttings.

Tarragon

A marvellous herbaceous perennial plant with subtle tasting leaves for flavoring many dishes including chicken, eggs, salads, and wine vinegar. French tarra-gon is available in pots, usually as small rooted cuttings, since seed is not available. Russian tarragon sets seed well, and this is the seed found in packet form; unfortunately it has a very poor flavor and is not a good herb.

French tarragon grows about 2–3ft, Russian 5–6½ft, and should be given a sunny spot, in patio paving, bed or container — of at least bucket size to let the clump develop. Plant in good soil or potting mix. Divide clumps every year or two, and this is the best way of increasing plants too.

Thyme

Culinary or French thyme is a fine little evergreen shrubby plant. Excellent as a gray-green edging to beds, however small, for underplanting shrubs in tubs, window boxes, pots and even hanging baskets. Thyme may be used in many ways including stews, sausage meat and egg dishes. Lemon thyme is similar but with a lemony flavor and variegated leaves. They grow 8–12in tall.

There are also a number of decorative thymes, usually prostrate and mat forming. They vary greatly in aromatic qualities, some are very good, others not, so test a leaf if you can before buying. Such thymes are really very good crack and crevice fillers.

All the thymes add to the atmosphere of a barbecue if a few pieces are sprinkled on the charcoal. Increase by cuttings.

Below A mixture of herbs planted informally in a free standing pot, gives a colorful and delicate summer display

INDEX

Picture credits

Molly Adams: 11 (cr)
Elly Arnstein/Stephen Sandon: 23 (b)
Carlo de Benedetti: 16 (t)
Steve Bicknell: 10 (tl, tr), 11 (tr,cl,b),
  14 (tl)
R. J. Corbin: 31 (tl,tr,b)
Brecht Einzig: 14 (c)
John Glover: 1, 21, 29
Lyn and Derek Gould: 23 (t), 25 (t,c),
  51, 63 (b), 71 (b), 72 (b), 87
Susan Griggs Agency: 9 Michael Boys,
  10 (cr)
Iris Hardwick Library: 84
Clive Helm: 14 (b)
P. Hunt: 35 (b), 47 (b)
George Hyde: 32
IMS: 14 (tr)
Bill McLaughlin: 8 (t,b)
Murphy Chemicals Co: 35 (t)
Rotaflex Home Lighting: 15
Harry Smith Horticultural Photographic
  Collection: 4, 12 (t), 17 (t), 18, 19 (b),
  20, 22 (t), 23 (b), 36, 38, 39, 41,
  42 (b), 43, 44, 45 (t,b), 46, 49, 50, 52,
  53, 54, 55, 56, 57, 59, 60, 61 (t), 64,
  65 (t), 66, 67 (b), 68, 69, 70 (t,b),
  71 (t), 73, 76 (l,r), 77, 78, 79, 82, 85
Wolfram Stehling: 10 (b), 12 (b), 13 (tr),
  19 (t)
Jerry Tubby: 16 (b)
Michael Warren: endpapers, 2/3, 5, 7,
  10 (cl), 11 (tl), 13 (tl,b), 17 (b), 22 (b),
  27, 37, 42 (t), 47 (t), 48, 58, 61 (b),
  62, 63 (t), 65 (b), 67 (t), 72 (t), 74, 75,
  81, 86